The Campcraft Book

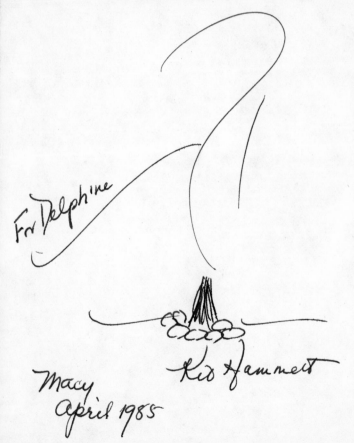

For Delphine

Kid Hammett

Macy
April 1985

The Campcraft Book

A Beginner's Guide to Outdoor Living Skills

Revised Edition

by

Catherine T. Hammett

Original Illustrations Revised by Rocky Oliver

American Camping Association
Martinsville, Indiana

First Printing, February 1981

Second Printing, July 1982

Hammett, Catherine Tilley.
The Campcraft Book.

Edition of 1950 published under title: Your
Own Book of Campcraft.
1. Outdoor Life.   2. Camping.   I. American
Camping Association.   II. Title.
GV191.7.H35   1980   796.54   80-26705

Contents

From the Author

Perhaps you have read stories of the people who lived in the early days of America—the Indians, explorers, and woodsmen. They were America's first campers; they have left people of today a heritage that makes them want to get out-of-doors, to know and enjoy the creatures and things that live there. They have left a challenge, too, to make good use of our camping lands and forests. Those of us who live in cities and towns have much to learn before we can enjoy to the fullest the woods and the out-of-doors. That learning is the beginning of the camp-craft trail.

This book is planned to help you develop those camp-craft skills that will make you a good camper. Each skill can lead to fascinating new trails and activities, either separately, or all woven together into one great adventure of camping.

Kit Hammett

Introduction

Nothing is as inspiring as being in the outdoors—and nothing is more fun if one knows how to live comfortably in the outdoors. In recent years, Americans have found that inspiration and fun in the parks, lakes and forest lands across our country. Since the mid-nineteenth century, organized camps have been helping persons of all ages gain an understanding of the outdoors and the skills to have fun there. Each year some 8,000,000 persons enjoy an organized camp experience.

It is appropriate that the American Camping Association, the only national accrediting body for all types of camps, brings back to the public the updated revision of the best known basic outdoor living skills guide, *Your Own Book of Campcraft.*

Catherine T. Hammett has been an active camper for over 60 years, gaining experience in Girl Scout camps, and moved from a position with a local council to the national staff of the Girl Scouts of the U.S.A., where she served in a variety of positions for a number of years.

"Kit" Hammett's skills in outdoor living and leadership training took her to all corners of the U.S.A., as well as to Latin America and Europe. Yet she found time to give of her volunteer services to American Camping Association locally and nationally, and eventually to serve as president of American Camping Association 1954-55. She was part of the task committee that developed ACA's Campcraft Program (changed to Outdoor Living Skills in 1977). This new edition carries the Campcrafter and Advanced Campcrafter skill requirements of that program.

However skilled a leader and author "Kit" may be, her greatest characteristic is her interest in people. That concern for people combined with the conviction that the essence of camping is getting to know and enjoy the outdoors in a democratic camp community comes through in her books.

The American Camping Association is proud to be able to present to campers everywhere this basic guide to outdoor living.

Armand B. Ball, Jr.
Executive Vice President
American Camping Association

1
"COME ON OUT!"

Come on out! Out for a picnic, out for a hike, out to go camping in the woods, out to cook a hamburger, or out just to be lazy under the sun and blue sky! Come on—let's go somewhere!

Did you ever bake a potato in the coals of an outdoor fire, eating it so hot you could hardly hold it? Did you ever spend the night in a tent, waking up sometime in the early morning to wonder at the brightness of the stars? Did you ever put a pack on your back, hike up hill and down and reach the end of the trail feeling tired, but oh so good? Did you ever sit around a campfire, singing or telling stories, while the fire crackled? If you have, it is a sure thing that you felt it was great fun; if you have never done any such things, it is just as sure that you've sometimes wished you could. Most of us are campers at heart and like nothing better than getting out-of-doors for the adventure that is there.

Hiking and camping give you many chances for the best of outdoor activities and fun. Whether you camp by a lake, go by canoe along quiet inland waterways, climb a mountain, ride a horse over prairie country, drive in your family's trailer to new camping land, or join some organized summer camping group, you know that living outdoors can be the best possible way of spending vacation time. But, outdoor fun can begin at home with your family, in your club or troop, and day trips to nearby spots can give you a taste of the adventure that is in store when you can go farther afield.

Perhaps you have read accounts of the people who lived in the early days of America—the Indians, the explorers, the woodsmen, the families of the covered wagon treks. They were America's first campers; they have left young people a heritage that makes them want to get out-of-doors, to know and enjoy the creatures and things that live there. They have left a challenge, too, to make good use of our natural resources, camping lands, and forests. Those of us who live in cities and towns have much to learn before we can enjoy to the fullest the woods and the out-of-doors, which were thoroughly familiar to this country's earliest settlers. We must begin to develop skills that will help us learn how to live outdoors. Some of us can go to summer camps, others can go camping with their families, and still others can find town hiking and exploring groups. But all must start with learning skills—and that learning is the beginning of the campcraft trail.

Every kind of game and sport has its experts and its beginners; in between, there are lots of people who are just average or a little better. None of them can say they are good at the game unless they know the rules and can play it skillfully. You don't wear a football helmet when you play tennis; you don't play baseball with hockey sticks; you don't serve in basketball; you don't kick off in archery; you don't make a run in bowling. Every sport or hobby has its particular rules of playing, its particular equipment, and its high standards of good performance. Camping has too; and, while many people may go outdoors and have a good time there, they are not considered good campers if they lack the knowledge of what to do and how to do it. In camping there are rules of the woods for good performance, equipment that brands you as an expert, tricks and skills that show you are knowledgeable. Good campers are concerned with conservation of natural resources; they know how to build fires easily, how to control them, how to cook a meal that is done to a turn. Campcraft is the art or skill of being a good camper; for most, campcraft means the very first things learned that lead to more advanced outdoor fun.

This book is planned to help you develop those campcraft skills that will make you a good camper. They are just the very first steps, but each can lead to fascinating

new trails and activities, either separately, or all woven
together into one great adventure of camping.

One thing about camping is that you seldom can do it
without bearing a real responsibility for other people or
property. You cannot go on a hike, build a fire, pitch a
tent, or follow a trail without using private and/or public
forests or parks of which we are the custodians. The
way we use these lands for camping has a relation to
other people. A good camper knows not only how to
make an outdoor fire, but how to control it; he knows
not only how to choose and set up a campsite; but how
to leave the site with no signs of a camper's presence.

Just as in tennis, or baseball, or photography, the
more you know, the more fun you have; in camping you
have many, many trails of adventure to follow as you
learn more of campcrafting and of forest lore. Here are
campcrafting ways to help you as you start down the
trails.

Where to Have Outdoor Fun

An Indian boy hunted and fished as part of his daily
living; learning to shoot a bow and arrow was part of his
schooling. Boys and girls of log cabin days helped to
build their homes and, as part of their everyday chores,
to get wood for the fire. Today we must go away from
home to hike, to camp, or to learn about nature. Many
people erroneously think they must go far away, and so
seldom have the fun they might have. There are good
outdoor places even in a city, and many chances to learn
outdoor skills indoors. Anyone can begin to learn about
camping, no matter where he may be—and when he
finds himself in real camping country, he will have a far
better time because of all he knows.

In the City

Get outdoors in the parks, or playgrounds, and in
yards. If you live in a small town or on the edge of a city,

you may have a spot where you and your club or troop can build a fireplace. If you have a club or troop, your meeting place may offer chances for some outdoor fun. Walks around the streets in suburban towns, visits to estates that have interesting trees and bushes, and day trips out of town to nearby parks and forests are always possible. In New York City there are camping sites on the roofs of skyscrapers; in Chicago you can get to a forest preserve from downtown in less than an hour's bus trip; in many smaller places you can get to open spaces on a fairly short walk. Don't let city streets and tall buildings keep you indoors! There are plenty of places to enjoy outdoor fun—anywhere!

In Camp

Some of you will have the chance to go camping—with your family, with your troop, with your club, or to a summer camp. You will find all sorts of chances for outdoor adventures there. The campcrafting skills that are mentioned here may help you to prepare yourself for a mountain trip of several days, a trip on horseback, or by canoe. When you do go to camp—whether for overnight or for many weeks—take the chance that is there to do *real* outdoor things, the things that are hard to do alone or in the city.

2
ON THE TRAIL

"I'm happy when I'm hiking, pack upon my back—,"
so goes a song that campers often sing as they swing
along the trail. Hiking is one of the best of outdoor
activities, perhaps because it combines so many parts of
outdoor fun—adventure, good exercise, outdoor cooking, trailing, exploring, and many others. There are all
sort of hikes; ranging from the short afternoon's walk to a
mountain climbing trip. In between lie many different
trails.

Planning

Individuals, families, camp groups, or in-town groups
get extra fun from making plans and preparations and
learning outdoor skills indoors on the days between
hikes. Most of us cannot get out into the country as often
as we would like, so it helps stretch outdoor fun to do
things beforehand. You can learn about interesting
things to be seen along the trail and you can develop

skills to help you enjoy the woods. You can pack and repack, to be sure you have just the right things to take—and you will find that well-laid plans will pay off in a better kind of a day once you are off.

Your very first hike may be the beginning of a hobby that will last a lifetime! So go at it right, from the beginning! There are many hiking, mountain, and trail clubs whose members have found new and interesting things to do out-of-doors. Some of these groups have national and local organizations with memberships available.

Hiking has been described as walking with a will; for campcrafters, it generally means getting about under your own steam, by foot, by bike, by horseback, in a canoe—generally in groups. As you grow in skill, you may advance to mountain or rock climbing. But for most of you, hiking will mean day trips, or perhaps an overnight camp, so these next pages will help with such first steps.

Why not get some hiking enthusiast to tell you some of his adventures? Or perhaps you can talk with someone who has gone hosteling, or on a canoe trip, or over a long horseback trail. Perhaps someone can show you slides or movies to help you catch the wonderful feeling of being away from everything, high on a hill or deep in the wilderness. Your first hikes will be setting the stage for just such adventures for you.

Many places where hikers and campers can go provide shelters and places to cook. American Youth Hostels, Delaplane, VA 22025, maintains such places at a very small cost; your group can get a group membership, or you may join as an individual. State and federal parks and forests often have camping spots or hiking places. Find out what there is that you can use, in your own town, or nearby—and begin to plan to make use of it all. There is no need to stay home!

Whether your family is going on a picnic, your troop on a Saturday hike, or your club off for a weekend trip to a summer cottage, someone will need to make plans. You'll be off to a bad start if you get to the meeting place and discover that half the group didn't know when to meet. It is worse to start preparing lunch only to discover that no one brought the meat. All this means—make a plan. Everyone who is going may have a hand in planning, or you may have several committees to do the planning; it's more fun for everyone to have a part in *some* of it. Here are some suggestions on what to think about:

For any hike or short trip, talk over and decide:

> where to go—when and how
> what to take
> how it will be packed and carried
> what to wear
> what to do on the way, and when you are at your campsite or trail
> how to divide jobs
> how to walk on the highway and preserve the area you are passing through.

If you are planning an overnight hike or camping trip, add these to the list given above:

> Who will be a contact person at home who knows your plans;
> Plan for well-balanced meals, including how to pack, carry, and store food;
> Plan for setting up your campsite, including shelter, equipment, how to make camp, how to leave it in its original condition;
> If you go to some place that has some equipment, find out details and secure the necessary permits before you complete your plans;
> Plan sleeping arrangements, including how to pack and carry;
> Plan personal equipment, including how to pack and carry.

Work up to an overnight trip. If your group has not done much hiking, plan several short or easy jaunts to help you get ready for a longer one. All your campcrafting skills will be put to a test on an overnight hike—so be sure you have the skills before you go. These steps will help you get ready.

Cook several different meals in your outdoor kitchen.

Go on at least one all-day hike—dressed properly, carrying your own food and equipment.

Sleep outdoors on the ground at least once, near camp or home.

Go on a two-meal trip or hike, carrying everything you need.

Learn to make a blanket roll and to pack your personal gear properly.

You should be ready by now!

Where to Go

There are a number of places to go. Some suggestions are:

—to *city parks, reservations, forests, or sanctuaries*.

—to *private property* where you can get permission to use the land. Groups may often have the use of a corner of someone's property as a permanent place for hikes and camps.

—to *camps* belonging to local organizations. (Ask around to see if there are any you may use.)

—by bus, car, or train to *state or federal parks or forests* where there may be trails for hiking, camping spots, or overnight shelters.

—just out in the *open country*, along dirt roads, off main highways. Local newspapers often outline such trips in the spring and fall; watch for such interesting items.

—to *points of historical or local interest*; get to know your own countryside.

To find out what is available, get in touch with local organizations and such agencies as park and recreation departments, state forest or park officials, and federal agencies, such as the U.S. Forest Service. Some organizations have suggestions for short day trips, giving information about things such as routes, and costs.

As far as possible—go under your own steam. Make it a hike!

What to Eat

See the chapter on *Outdoor Food* for this—whether you plan to carry your lunch ready-made, or to cook it on the trail.

What to Take

This depends on what you plan to do. For a day's trip, take a ready-made lunch or food to make sandwiches or to cook on the spot. For other equipment—a knife, a first aid kit, a cup, a notebook, a sketchbook or your camera, a map, and a compass may be the things you will need.

If you are cooking, take matches, cooking utensils, and tools you will need.

Pack your lunch and equipment in a day pack, which can be carried over your shoulder or on your back. Let your hands be free to help you swing along the trail.

You may need permission for using fireplaces or for building fires in certain areas at certain times of the year. There may also be regulations as to the type of fuel that can be used and how it may be secured. Check with the area where you are thinking of camping to be sure about this. When picnic places are crowded, it is sometimes wise to secure a permit in advance to be sure you will have a place.

Be sure to ask permission before crossing or using private property.

Plan for a safe water supply. If it will not be available at your campsite, plan to take it with you. (If you need information on how to purify water, write the Center for Disease Control, Atlanta, GA 30333 for their pamphlet, "Safe Drinking Water in Emergencies.")

What to Wear

This, too, depends on what you are going to do, as well as on the climate, season, and the probable weather for the day. Mainly, it is important just to use your head. Avoid too much or too little; too much will be a burden, too little will have painful results, and either will spoil your fun. Get advice from the experts in your locality.

Old, comfortable clothes that help you enjoy the outdoors with freedom of action and freedom from care are the best. Wear things that won't get snagged, that are strong but light, and that tend to be roomy rather than tight.

In general—plan for the kind of activity and the kind of weather you are likely to have.

In the *fall*, the days will be warm, but as soon as the sun goes down you'll need a sweater or jacket.

In the *winter*, several lightweight layers will keep you warmer than one very heavy layer, and you can take layers off or put them back on as you need them.

When moving in the *sun*, keep head, shoulders, and legs covered (go at sun-tanning gradually!). Peel off shirts when resting in the shade. Wear sunglasses when on the road.

For *cross-country* or rough going, wear jeans or smooth-material pants that won't catch burrs; protect arms and legs from briars and branches.

For *snow*, wear lightweight, warm ski or snow clothes. Most body heat is lost from the head and the extremities of the arms and legs. Mittens are warmer than gloves with individual fingers—an underlayer of wool adds warmth. Wear two pairs of socks with heavy boots—one pair should be wool or a thermal type since this is the only material which will hold warmth when wet. Plan extra socks for the time when you come indoors again; wear waterproof boots.

For *wind*, wear closely woven jackets and pants with close-fitting cuffs at wrists and ankles, and a scarf at your neck.

For *rain*, in the summer it probably doesn't matter—if you can, change to dry clothes when you stop walking. For cooler days, put a lightweight rainjacket or coat in your pack. Water-repellent jackets serve many purposes and are especially useful for unexpected showers. Plan something to cover your head, and to keep rain from going uncomfortably down your neck.

For *hiking*, wear footgear that is comfortable (not new), that gives good support, and is adequate for the terrain you are covering. The boots or shoes should be roomy, but not too large; wear two pairs of socks.

For *bicycling*, long hair should be tied back or covered to keep it from blowing. Pants or jeans with wide legs should be tied or tucked in at the ankles. Keep knees covered on first jaunts in sun.

For *mountain climbing* and more advanced activities, get advice before you begin to build your camping wardrobe.

For *overnight camping* trips, go as light as you can; use T-shirts and cutoffs or jeans and take extra socks and a jacket (suitable for weather) and underwear.

What to Do on the Way or When You Arrive

This depends, too, on where you go and what is around; but, in general, make the most of being out-of-doors, and do the things you can't do in town or in other seasons.

See what there is to see—of historical, local, or natural interest. Look up nature trails, scenic views, museums, and wildlife exhibits.

Plan time on the way to see around you—the scenery, the people, the birds, and trees and insects. A hike offers great chances for this—don't speed along as if you were off for a big trip.

If you are planning a particular destination, chart your time along the way so you can do these things. Go

and return by different routes if you can. Plan your return trip; it is part of the hike and the way back always seems longer.

If you plan to stay at one spot for most of the day, you will want to get there in the most direct fashion and plan for the time there to learn new skills, cook something that takes some time, sit around and talk, or play games. Be ready to change everything if some fine new adventure turns up; you may have a chance to watch some ants moving their homes, or playing games may be such fun you don't want to stop—being outdoors means leisurely hours, just to have fun.

Dividing Jobs

If everyone tries to make the fire, help cook, and lead in games, confusion will result. Besides, not everybody needs to be working all the time, so some can play games, sit by the brook, climb trees, or skip stones while others are doing the jobs that need to be done. Unless you know what your share is, though, you don't always feel free to wander off, or sit and read. Dividing up jobs is the answer.

Some people make charts that give everyone a job; others count off, assigning jobs to numbers; others like to let people choose, being sure that making the fire does not always go to the expert, but rather to those who need to learn how. Cleaning up is always the least pleasant job, but some provision needs to be made for that; it really should be everyone's job, and if everyone is careful not to throw things around, there isn't much to be done. When there is a crowd, you may divide something like this:

Fire Makers—Arrange fireplace, woodpile, etc. Make and tend fire. (Generally everyone else gets wood, first thing.) Put out the fire when finished.

Cooks—Prepare and serve meals, or arrange food out of the way of insects, animals, and humans. Each person can get his own when it is time to eat. For big crowds, divide into groups of three or four to cook and eat together. Or, you may divide again and have another group, apart from the cooks, that arranges the table for food and utensils.

Program—There may be need of a group to plan the activities of the day, to lead in these activities, to plan the campfire, etc.

Clean-ups—Even when everyone pitches in, there needs to be a special squad to supervise and plan how it will be done. They see that the site is left better than they found it; they check to be sure the fire is out, the rubbish taken care of.

When planning for any kind of hike or camp, plans should be made beforehand about what will happen when you first reach the site. Generally, the campsite is organized for the day; food put away in a cool, dry, insect-free place; fire areas and cooking places put in readiness; jackets and other equipment stored in a dry place.

For overnight camps, this is even more necessary; get the most important group necessities taken care of—the cooking place, food storage place, shelters for night, latrine and washing place. Divide the jobs into those that one or two do for the group, and those that each camper does for himself.

If you make plans for a hike with your club or group, the plans may look something like this:

Where We'll Go—Destination

How long will it take to get there?
How do we go? (Hike all the way?
   Bus part way? etc.)
Time to leave
Time to return
Cost, if any
File plan with contact person at home

What We'll Do— On the way
At the site
On the way home

What Should We Learn Beforehand?

What to Take?	**Food**	**Equipment**
Who Will Bring?		**Menu Planned**
Program supplies or equipment		

Who Will Do What?	**Check List for Each Person**
Wood gatherers	money?
Fire builders	food?
Cooks	equipment?
Clean-ups	knife?
	compass?
	personal gear?

3
YOUR OWN
OUTDOOR EQUIPMENT

You begin to collect your own camping and hiking equipment when you get your first pocket knife. Much of your equipment you can assemble or make yourself; there are many kinds that you will buy. It's the campcrafting way to make your own—even small tents and sleeping bags. Such pieces of equipment are more advanced than those discussed in this book, but you will want to progress to them.

What You Need

A *bandana handkerchief* is a campcrafter's best friend as a sweat band, a towel, something to wrap your lunch in, something to hold things you are bringing home.

You'll want a bright one to hang on your belt, or tuck in your pants.

A *hike kit* will come next—a day pack with shoulder straps for your back. Make one out of good, heavy material like denim or rip-stop nylon. Make it big enough to fit your plate and cup and little frying pan. Put pockets in it for your lunch or your knife and fork. Make it sturdy—for hard use. Stitch on a sewing machine, or use strong cord and a large needle.

Have your hike kit ready for any occasion—it will be easier to get going if it is all ready, hanging on a peg, just waiting for an outdoor day.

Little *bags*, with clothesline drawstring tops, called ditty bags, for food or personal equipment are good to make, too.

Leather *sheaths* for knives and axes are good craft projects.

A *first aid kit* is a necessity for any outing. Knowledge of what to do is necessary, too. Plan your kit to take care of things that may happen, and talk with a nurse or first aider to tell you how to treat cuts, scratches, bruises, burns, and sprains. You can make your own first aid kit or buy one ready-made.

If you plan overnight hikes and camping, you will need a *waterproof ground sheet*. You may buy or borrow a poncho, or a piece of heavy plastic or waterproofed cloth that can be used as a ground sheet. You can waterproof your own with waterproofing liquid (purchased at hardware stores) or by rubbing with paraffin, then pressing with a hot iron.

You will want small *tents* for one camper. Many types of tents can be purchased at little cost at army surplus stores, catalog houses, or outdoor equipment companies. It is an advanced project to make your own.

A *sleeping bag* or *blanket roll* will complete your sleeping arrangements.

As you and your group grow more experienced, you may make pack baskets, knapsacks, pack boards, paddles, bicycle packs, and many other things you will need.

There's no feeling like that proud feeling of a good, well-made piece of equipment—something that you have made yourself!

Learn to take good care of your equipment, store it away after each trip; it will repay you many times.

Talk with people who go camping every year; they will tell you how much planning is put into their equipment. They will tell you what they think is important, and can help you know what to begin to collect as your camping and hiking gear.

When you and your family begin to get camping gear for a family trip, you'll want easily transportable items that will fit into your trailer or the trunk of your car.

Your group may make a start at equipment, jointly made and owned. Lightweight tents, boxes that carry food and then become cupboards, nested kettles—all will be considered in your planning.

For canoe trips, horseback trips, and mountain climbing trips, you'll want specialized equipment that you can pack and carry with ease. Talk to experts on this.

Making a Blanket Roll

For an overnight hike or for any camping trip, prepare your bed at home before starting out. An envelope or Klondike bed keeps you warm because you have blankets under and over you—and you cannot kick them off. Use this method for any cold night, indoors or out.

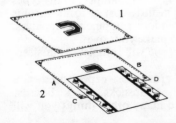

1. Place poncho flat on ground.

2. Place first blanket with one edge down center of poncho. (A-B)

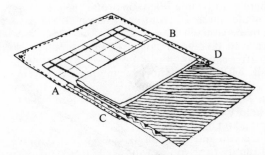

3. Place second blanket with one edge at *middle* of first blanket. (C-D)

4. Alternate blankets in same way, until all are down. Fold sheet or sleeping blanket in half, and place in middle. (A-B-C-D)

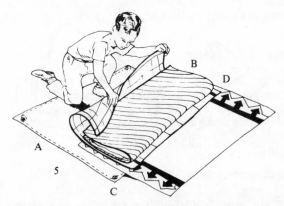

5. Starting with last blanket you put down, fold blankets, alternating in reverse order, until all are over middle. (A-B-C-D)

Pin with blanket pins at bottom, if poncho does not snap together, or fold under.

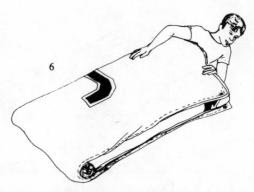

6. Fold poncho over. Snap together, if there are snaps on bottom and side.

Wriggle down from the top, getting in the middle of the sleeping blanket or sheet.

7. When packing up, put your night things and toilet articles inside and roll from bottom.

See page 102 for knots to tie the roll.

Sleeping bags for camping out come in a variety of sizes, shapes, materials, and weights. The kind you buy depends on the style you wish, the amount of money you wish to invest, and the season of the year you plan to use it. Visit an outdoor equipment store or ask for help from an experienced camper before you purchase your bag.

4
CAMPCRAFT SKILLS

No matter how much you like outdoor fun, you can't learn everything at once, so start with simple steps and progress along the trail in easy stages. Just in case you may not know where to begin or how to find the easy stages, here are some tests that will help you. Many camps have similar tests that are planned especially for the kinds of things that can happen around that particular camp; some organizations have outdoor tests for badges or honors. If you do not have such help in your camp or your organization, there is a program of progressive Outdoor Living Skills by the American Camping Association that is available. There are two steps in the program for beginners: Campcrafter and Advanced Campcrafter. You may work on them on your own or with a group. If you wish to be certified as a Campcrafter or Advanced Campcrafter and be authorized to wear the patches for either level, courses are available in most areas and are taught by Certified Outdoor Living Skills Instructors. Write to the American Camping Association at the address shown in the organization listing at the end of the book for information on courses near where you live.

If your family is planning to go camping next summer, you all may like to work on some progressive steps together. If your club or school grade is planning a camping experience, or if you and your group want to see how well you can measure up against each other, you will find these helpful.

Campcrafter

Prerequisites:

This rating is for beginners interested in acquiring **basic** outdoor living skills. Trainees must be at least twelve years old or indicate previous experience and ability to accomplish basic outdoor living skills.

While the requirements are simple, it is assumed that the tests will be carried out with high standards of skills, adequacy, and competence.

Requirements:

Toolcraft

Demonstrate ability to handle, care for, and store pocketknife.

Ropecraft

Know various types of rope and demonstrate proper care of rope.

Demonstrate ability to:

1. Whip a rope
2. Tie and use one each of the following types of knots: joining, stopper, loop, end-securing, bowline, overhand, taut line hitch, clove hitch.

Gear and Shelter

Demonstrate selection, packing and carrying of personal gear suitable for locality including clothing, program, safety items, shelter, sleeping for one-day or an overnight trip.

Share in selecting, packing, and carrying group gear for a one-day or an overnight trip.

Make an item of individual gear or set up a simple shelter.

Health and Safety

State ten health practices and ten safety practices in relation to outdoor living activities.

Demonstrate use of good health and safety practices.

Outline preventive measures and first-aid procedures for common emergencies in hiking and outdoor living.

Describe benefits and health factors in personal cleanliness.

Map and Compass

Demonstrate ability to:

1. Read a compass by giving bearings to designated objects.
2. Find direction by the sun and stars.
3. Give and follow simple directions using sketch map, trail signs, etc.
4. Use compass in a field project.

Nature and Conservation

Consider the effects of your outdoor living practices upon the environment at all times.

Be able to identify the major poisonous or harmful plants or animals found in the locality and know precautions and treatment for same.

Indicate three good conservation practices in immediate camp or trip area.

Indicate three violations of good conservation.

Campsite

Learn to locate a suitable site for the number of people camping.

Consider all the functions you will need and set up a site to best advantage.

In some established or outpost sites it is best to use the same fire scar, waste water, and latrine sites all season. In such cases, leave them intact until the last use. Justify your decisions.

Firecraft

Select and prepare a firesite for charcoal or artificial logs, a camp stove, and a wood fire.

Choose and learn to operate and care for one type of camp stove.

Learn how to light, utilize, and extinguish various fuels for future use.

Where possible, select and store supply of natural materials for a fire. Build a foundation or beginning fire and keep it going for several minutes.

Discuss and observe safety and conservation practices.

Food

Plan, prepare, and pack a balanced trail lunch requiring no cooking and a well-balanced meal demonstrating three types of simple outdoor cooking.

Discuss how to camp simply.

Leadership

Work out a plan for helping campers to acquire similar skills including camper participation in planning and carrying out a day's trip.

All Day Trip

Share in planning for, carrying out, and evaluating a day or overnight trip away from the living area; include one meal with two types of outdoor cooking.

Demonstrate practice of personal hygiene and camp sanitation.

ADVANCED CAMPCRAFTER

Prerequisites:

This rating is for campers who have had some previous experience in outdoor living. It is designed to follow the Campcrafter rating or equivalent skills. The steps in the Advanced Campcrafter are **in addition** to those in Campcrafter.

Requirements:

Toolcraft

Discuss need for careful use of tools, to learn how to use tools properly, to check on local regulations concerning tool use.

Demonstrate ability to:

1. Set up a chopping and sawing area.
2. Sharpen an axe and knife.
3. Saw a log into short lengths and split it for kindling.
4. Chop a log into two parts.
5. Cut off and trim a tree limb where possible.

Ropecraft

Identify different fibers and their uses.
Demonstrate ability to:

1. Tie and use four knots.
2. Make a length of rope.
3. Make one type of splicing.
4. Use three types of lashing. Use for a project or in setting up campsite.

Gear and Shelter

Demonstrate ability to:

1. Select, pack, and carry personal gear for an overnight camping trip.
2. Erect some type of temporary shelter from materials you brought with you.

Share in the making of an item of group gear.

Health and Safety

Demonstrate a method of purifying water supply for drinking and for cooking.

List common emergencies possible in outdoor living in your locality, and plan a first aid kit to take care of such emergencies on a trip.

Have first aid training and discuss problem situations.

Map and Compass

Make a simple topographic map of your campsite.
Share in laying out a meaningful compass course of several points. Follow a similar course.
Demonstrate ability to:

1. Orient and read a topographic map and four other kinds of maps.
2. Measure heights and distances by personal measurements.

Nature and Conservation

Identify several types of native material in an outdoor living program for the locality.
Demonstrate interest in and awareness of the common natural resources of area.
Share in working out some type of project to stimulate interest in the out-of-doors.
Indicate knowledge of weather signs significant to good camping in the area.

Campsite Selection

Complete Campsite Selection Requirements.

Firecraft

Demonstrate ability to:

1. Build a charcoal, presto log, etc., fire and cook on it.
2. Light, use, and care for several different camp stoves. Cook on one.
3. Prepare a firesite and a fire for cooking, warmth, and fellowship.
4. Identify common woods of the area and know their burning qualities.

Food

Plan, prepare, and pack a balanced trail meal using concentrated food requiring no cooking.

Share in setting up a trail kitchen for overnight or longer.

Demonstrate three types of outdoor cooking.

Share in planning menu and food list for a two-day trip including dehydrated and easily packed foods. Consider the quantity of water needed and its sources.

Overnight or Longer Trip

Share in planning for, carrying out, and evaluating an overnight or longer camping trip away from the living area; include at least two meals.

Demonstrate practice of personal hygiene and camp sanitation.

Leadership

Discuss and review all aspects to leadership principles and techniques covered in the course and their application to work with campers.

Work out a plan for helping campers to acquire skills covered in this course including camper participation in planning and carrying out an overnight trip.

No list can ever be made to meet all the varying conditions and situations in all parts of the country and in all camps and groups. If you find that something is much more important in your section, or more interesting because of what grows there, or the kind of country it is, substitute that in place of what is here. If you are a member of a club or camp or group, you may want to make up a whole new set of activities. There are many, many more skills and activities to beckon you on down the campcraft trail.

Have fun!

5
FIRE BUILDING AND FIREPLACES

Fire—your good friend and servant in the out-of-doors.
There is nothing a campcrafter enjoys more, or uses
more, than a fire—from that glowing campfire to sit
around in the dark to the quick, hot fire that boils water.
Fire is a good servant when under control. So, while ap-
preciating all a fire does, it is important to realize what
you must do to control it. Care of the fire and fire
prevention become *responsibilities* of anyone who lights
a match in the open—and so a good campcrafter knows
not only how to light a fire, but also how to put it out.

Fire has many uses: to cook food, heat water, destroy
rubbish, and give warmth. A campcrafter learns to
make a beginning or foundation fire, and how to build
it into different types of fires for various uses. In many

outdoor places, charcoal or camp stoves must be used because open fires are not permitted or fuel is not available.

A good fire

1. is built in a safe place which helps control it;
2. is just large enough to serve the need and to make thrifty use of fuel.
3. is kept under control, and is watched at all times;
4. is put out when no longer needed.

Fires may be made of wood that can be found in the outdoors; but in some places such as public parks, one is required to use charcoal. In other places where wood is not readily available, charcoal is used, wood is carried in, or camping stoves are used.

Here are steps to take in learning to build a fire.

1. Fix a place for building the fire.
2. Learn the kinds of materials used in firebuilding, and gather a big handful of each (enough to keep the fire going three minutes—so you need not leave the fire once it is lighted).
3. Build a *foundation* fire; and
4. Keep it going and build into a *tepee* or *crisscross* fire, and use it to toast food.
5. As soon as you are through with it, put it out.
6. Unless you build in a ready-made fireplace, leave no trace of your fire.
7. Practice many times—in the wind and in the rain— until you are sure you can light fires. (You may need to learn to light a match and let it get going before you put it in the fire. Practice this, too.)
8. Have someone with you when lighting a fire.

Step 1—Fixing a Fireplace

Where to Build

—On sand, rocks, or dirt. (Never at the base of a tree, or near enough for heat to kill the roots.) Ground should be cleared of leaves, grass, sticks, down to solid dirt, over a large enough area unless a stone fireplace is used. This is especially important in the woods. Clear away anything such as leaf mold to prevent fire from smoldering underground. If grass, undergrowth, or pine needles are found where you are going to build a fire, use a small shovel to cut out a circle of the top sod (the size of the fire area). Lift out the sod and set it aside to be replaced when you have finished with the fire area and extinguished the fire. (If the sod does contain growth, and you use the fire area longer than a few hours, water the sod occasionally to keep it from dying.)

—In a fireplace, temporary or permanent. Temporary fire places are made of ditches or holes dug in dirt, rocks, bricks, clay, or tin cans.

—With the wind at your back, as you face the fire. This will make a draft that blows *through* the fire when it is lighted.

Step 2—Materials to Use

Three types of materials are used in fires: tinder, kindling, and fuel.

Tinder: Material which catches fire from a match.

Should be in pieces not any thicker than a match, but longer. Shavings or fuzz sticks, fine twigs (especially from evergreen trees), bundles of tops of bushes or weeds, pieces of fat pine, or thin pieces of bark make good tinder. (Paper, of course, but campcrafters scorn it except in great emergencies.) Beware of light material like grass or leaves; these flare up quickly but have little real substance and burn out too quickly to catch on anything heavier.

Kindling: Good dry sticks and twigs graduated in size

from pieces just bigger than tinder up to pieces as thick as a thumb, and from six to twelve inches long. Larger pieces may split for kindling.

Fuel: The real fire material. Good, firm pieces of wood,

graduated in size from pieces just bigger than kindling up to good-sized logs, depending on use. Charcoal is often used as a fuel, too.

Learn each kind; be able to find some of each and keep it handy in a good woodpile, either a small temporary one or a larger, more permanent one.

A *good woodpile* is a convenience, as well as a safety device. Stack wood so that tinder, kindling, and fuel are in separate piles for convenience. Place woodpile near fireplace for convenience, but far enough away so you do not have to walk in it to get around the fire, and far enough away on the side away from the wind so that sparks cannot possibly fly into it.

Many kinds of fire starters can be easily made at home to help you in fire building. For a simple, easily-carried fire starter, you will need paraffin wax and cardboard egg cartons. Melt the wax in the top of a double boiler and watch the wax carefully as it melts. If it gets too hot, it will catch fire. If you wish, line each of the cups in the egg carton with small pieces of wood shavings . . . or put in a string to act as a wick for lighting. Carefully pour the liquid wax in each of the cups; any excess may be poured in the top of the carton for additional starting material. Allow the wax to harden and cool; close the top of the carton and your starters are ready to travel with you. As needed, tear off egg cups or portions of the top to help light your fire. Another starter is to shave old candles and wrap a small amount in a piece of waxed paper. Twist both ends to hold the shavings securely.

Kinds of Wood to Use

You will probably be using whatever you find around when you first begin to light fires. As you progress, you will learn about certain types of wood and which are best for certain purposes. Following are a few hints to help you make a woodpile that will be useful.

—Wood for kindling should snap when broken. In general, dead branches from lower limbs of trees make the best kindling. Sticks lying on the ground may be damp.

—Tinder may be anything that is very light and dry, not any thicker than a match. Make little bundles of tiny twigs.

—Sticks that *bend* and do not snap are green; use only after a hot fire is started.

—Wood that crumbles is rotten. (You'll find lots around—don't bother with it.) It has lost all its life and will just smoulder and smoke without giving off any heat.

—Split wood burns well; the inside of a log is drier than the outside.

—In wet weather, depend on dead branches on trees; they dry sooner than wood on the ground, as the air can get all around them.

Soft wood is produced by trees that grow quickly—pines, spruces, cedars, gray birch, and aspen. This wood is good for starting fires, or for quick, hot fires. It burns up quickly and needs constant refueling; it does not leave good coals.

Hard wood is produced by trees that grow slowly—oaks, hickories, yellow birch, maples, ash, mesquite, and eucalyptus. Hard wood is compact and firm, and feels heavy in the hand as compared with a piece of soft wood of the same size. This kind of wood burns slowly and yeilds coals that will last. It needs a good, hot fire to get started, and then burns well for a long time.

Visit a woodpile somewhere, and look over the wood. Try picking up a few pieces to see if you can tell which are *hard* and which are *soft*. Pick out some that will split for good kindling, some that will make good coals for broiling, some that will be good to burn in a fireplace on a cold day. What kinds of wood or other fuel are found around where you live?

Step 3—Start with a Foundation Fire

How to Build a Foundation Fire

1. Have fireplace ready before you begin.

2. Have ready, at hand:
   —a big handful of tinder
   —a double handful of kindling
   —the fuel you will need, unless there are wood-gatherers working with you so you will not have to leave the fire after it is lighted.

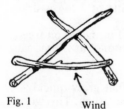

Fig. 1   Wind

3. Kneel with wind at your back; take two small sticks of kindling and place to form an angle in fireplace, as shown in Fig. 1; *or* place one stick across these two, to form an A.

Light here.

Fig. 2

4. Pile a good bit of tinder in the angle of the sticks, or on crosspiece, lightly, so there is air, but compactly enough so each piece rests against other pieces. Leave a tunnel at *center* and *bottom* in which to insert match. (Fig. 2.)

Fig. 3

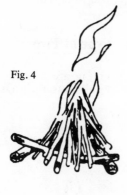

Fig. 4

Remember: Fire needs air. Flame burns *upward*. Only material in the path of flame will ignite.

5. Strike match, tipping down, so flame catches on wood. (Cup in hands if necessary.) When well lighted, stick flame in air space, putting flame under the *center* of the pile of tinder. If match goes out, use it as extra tinder. Blow gently at *base* of fire if necessary. (Fig. 3)

6. As flame catches and begins to spread, add bits of tinder, placing gently *on flame* until there is a brisk fire. (Fig. 4)

7. Then begin to add pieces of kindling, one by one, starting with small pieces, and gradually adding bigger pieces, placing lightly where the flame is best, forming a tepee shape. Do not make any *sudden* changes in size of wood used; add pieces that are just a bit larger than those already burning until you are using thumb-sized sticks. Hold stick at one end, placing hand near bottom of fire; let top of stick drop into flames.

Remember: Build gradually. Keep fire compact, each piece of wood touching other pieces for most of its length. Increase size of wood gradually.

8. Put a small stick or poker in bottom of fire to raise just a little, to give more air.

9. When fire is going well, begin to add fuel in graduated sizes, building into the kind of a fire you will need.

Step 4—Build into Some Type of Fire

Fire Building Hint: Tender and kindling are key elements—use to get a fire started, then build into the type of fire desired.

Cooking Fires

Tepee or Wigwam Fire
   This is a quick, hot fire for things like boiling that concentrates heat at a small point at top.
   Start with a foundation fire. Continue building with fuel in tepee formation, as shown, keeping it tall, not widespread.

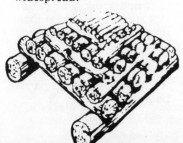

Crisscross Fire
   This is a solid fire that will burn to coals, or produce a long-burning fire.
   Start with foundation fire. Add fuel, as shown,

to make a crisscross of sticks. Put thick sticks at bottom after foundation fire is going very well, lighter sticks across.

Reflector Fire

This will provide high and steady heat for such things as baking and planking.

Start with a foundation fire and build it into a high crisscross fire in front of a rock or a reflector made of logs. Let it burn to good goals. For quick browning, build a high fire—as high as the top of the reflector or plank. If a large rock is not available, pile some small ones up to make the reflecting wall at the back of your fire. Brace the rocks from the back with logs. If sufficient rocks are not found, build your own reflector out of aluminum foil and use sticks, dowels, or coathangers for the upright poles. The vertical holders should be as tall as the fire. Place the uprights to form a long screen in the back of the fire and angle the two sides to protect the side area. Secure the long piece of foil by wrapping it around one of the uprights pushed into the ground; always put the shiny side to the fire for better reflection. Stretch the side pieces of foil from the back poles to the angled ones which cover the sides. (This also makes a good wind protector for your fire if the day is windy enough to interfere with the burning.)

Reflector Ovens to Be Used with Reflector Fire

Ovens which utilize reflected heat are used with this type of fire. One which folds flat when not in use can be purchased at any camping equipment store; they are usually made of aluminum or stainless steel and are easy to use for baking and are easy to carry. Or, one can easily be made from a cardboard box: use a square box cut in half diagonally; cover the inside of the box with heavy-duty foil and use lengths of coathangers (remove the coating) from side to side in the middle of the box to form a shelf; lay the foil over the whole width of the shelf and wrap around the end pieces. Prop the oven up in back with rocks or sticks to slant the shelf at the best angle to catch the heat.

Air Space

Trench Fire

To provide long, narrow fire for trench-type fireplace, start with one or more foundation fires, and when going well, knock flat, instead of building into tepee. Make a long, narrow crisscross type, with long sticks the length of firebox, and small sticks crosswise, to provide air.

If fire seems to burn poorly, be sure you have plenty of air going in at the front. Raise sticks by a cross stick, if needed, in front. If you use rocks, be sure they are solid, not layered (shale), since the latter can shatter when hot.

Fire for Vagabond Stove

This is a small, steady fire in a stove made of a tin can.

Start with a small fire of tinder. Have a supply of sticks no bigger than thumb-size (for a #10 stove). Keep fire small, and *feed steadily* with small twigs. It needs plenty of air; keep extra tinder handy for bolstering up.

Move can in place when fire is going. Tin can cookery needs two persons—one to cook, the other to feed fire. The stove can be made from an open #10 can. Using tin snips, cut a square opening extending about halfway up the height of the can at the open end. Punch two holes with a punch can opener on opposite sides at the top for a draft. As an alternate fuel for the vagabond stove, a buddy burner can be used. Begin with a small can, such as one for tuna fish, and cut a strip of corrugated cardboard a little shorter than the height of the can. Wind the strip in a loose coil and place inside the can. Pour melted paraffin wax into the can until it is almost full. Allow to cool completely before touching. Place the stove over the burner and light it when you are ready to cook. When you are ready to extinguish the flame, put a flat piece of tin slightly larger than the diameter of the buddy burner on the top to smother the flame.

Charcoal Fires

In areas where wood fires are prohibited, wood is not available, or where ground fires are not allowed, charcoal in some type of stove may be used as a substitute. A charcoal fire will burn for a very long time and needs little refueling. Start a charcoal fire twenty to thirty minutes before you are ready to cook. Chemical or liquid starters for charcoal are dangerous and hard to handle; instead, use the foundation fire or the paraffin fire starters, or prepare your charcoal with paraffin before you leave home. Take a cardboard egg carton and put a small amount of briquet pieces in each cup. Pour the melted wax over the pieces and allow to remain until the wax is completely cool. With the top of the carton closed, you have a convenient container. To use, simply tear off the briquets you wish to use.

Tin Can Charcoal Stove

To make the stove, use a punch can opener to put a series of holes around the open top of the can and around the bottom. Stick ends of wire through two of the holes at the top and twist to make a handle. Take a piece of wire screen, curl it into a circle and secure it with wire. Place in the bottom of the can and put another circle of flat wire across it for a grate. Another grate on the top will allow you to use the can as a stove for frying, or use it to ignite briquets that you are going to transfer to another stove. After the briquets have been lighted, swing the stove gently by the handle to get them burning more quickly.

Charcoal Box Oven

Charcoal briquets also may be used for baking in a box oven. The oven can be made from a heavy cardboard carton and used again and again. A square box generally works well; the rule is that your box should be large

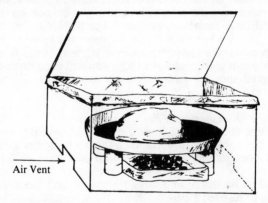

Air Vent

enough so that your cooking pan is three inches away from the side walls of the box in any direction. Cover the inside of the box and the underside of the top flap with heavy-duty foil. At the middle of the box on two sides opposite each other and at the spot where the side joins the bottom of the box, cut a small flap two or three inches wide (leaving it attached at the top of the cut so that it may be opened or closed). The flap is left open to provide extra air for the charcoal, and may be adjusted on a very windy day. Light your charcoal briquets in a charcoal stove; when glowing, place in a small foil pan about the same length and width of your cooking pan. Put the pan in the center of the bottom floor of the box; close the lid to preheat the oven. If you know the temperature at which the food should cook and wish to know how hot the oven is, put a small oven thermometer in the box. The temperature of the oven is controlled by the number of briquets you use—generally, each briquet used supplies forty degrees of heat.

If you are baking anything with a leavening agent (bread, cake, cookies, or pies), place four empty soup cans in the oven as the platform to hold your cooking pan. (The charcoal in its foil pan is between these cans on the floor of the box.) If you are cooking a meat dish or a casserole, use tuna fish cans at the corners so that your dish is closer to the heat. The cooking time for your dish in a box oven is usually about the same as that for comparable temperature in a kitchen oven. If the day is particularly cold or windy, you will need to find a sheltered spot for your box oven to maintain the heat more efficiently.

Putting Out Charcoal Fires

When you have finished your cooking, sprinkle water over the burning briquets—turn them with tongs so that both sides get thoroughly wet—until they are completely out and cool. Then put them in the sun to dry out; they can then be stored in a large tin can or safe place until ready to be used again.

Campfires

Campfires generally are laid some time before using, so the foundation fire must be sureproof, and the other structure in place before lighting.

Put plenty of tinder and kindling in the foundation fire. Add a wax fire starter for quick flaring. Arrange standing sticks over it, leaving an opening to insert lighted match. The trick is to be *sure* that there is *plenty of tinder and small kindling* and a place to insert the

Crisscross Fire

Tepee Fire

first light. In ceremonials, it is better to use extra tinder than to have the fire lighting keep every one in a frenzy of anxiety.

Altar fire

This is a special fire for ceremonials. It looks well in a fireplace, and is thrilling to watch as it burns. It goes against the old theory that fire burns up, but works if there is plenty of light stuff to ignite lower layers.

Make a long crisscross-type fire. On the top build one or two tepee fires, with leaders running down through

Altar Fire

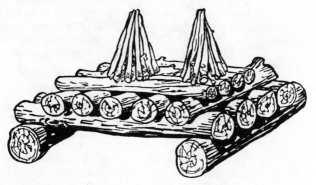

the inside of the crisscrosses. Use *plenty* of tinder and small stuff to make the rest catch.

Light the tepees and the fire will spread out and down until all is burning.

This type of fire should not need refueling throughout an evening.

Indoor fireplace fire

This may be a modification of either a tepee or a crisscross fire, generally built against a large back log.

Be sure there is enough small stuff and graduated sizes of wood to ignite the big logs. Once the fire is burning well, you can add logs. Keep the ashes in the bottom of fireplace; they conserve heat and help fill in air space. Or you can build a base fire of plenty of tinder and kindling and add crisscross and three logs on top; light from underneath. Use three commercial ready-light logs for a small campfire.

Garbage Disposal

Usually you must put garbage in containers provided or carry it out of the camp. If you can dispose of garbage by burning, here are some suggestions.

Build a good, freely burning crisscross fire, and pile garbage lightly on top. Drain as much as possible beforehand, and add a bit at a time, not all at once. When fuel is limited, dry garbage in the sun before burning.

It takes a good fire to burn garbage, which is generally very moist and needs heat to dry out. Provide plenty of air, too.

For a permanent garbage burning place, use a grill raised on stones or brick, allowing the fire room to burn without being smothered. Pile garbage lightly on grill. When burning papers, bundle into hard balls to prevent them from blowing away when lighted. Tear paper boxes into small pieces, and add gradually to fire.

Step 5—Put It Out

As soon as you are through cooking, or whatever you are doing with the fire, begin to put it out. This is especially important if you are out for the day and must go away and leave the spot later.

(a) Let fire die down as much as possible.
(b) Scatter coals, break up big pieces, knock logs apart.
(c) Stir coals—and *sprinkle* with water—then stir again. Repeat until there are no live coals—under the logs or in the middle.
(d) If you have no water, put on sand or dirt, and stir thoroughly.
(e) When you can press your hand on the spot where the fire was, you know it is out.
(f) Cover with dirt. If you have removed the top sod, replace and tamp down.

Fire Safety Hints

—Don't build fires when you are alone.
—Don't play with fire.
—Use fireplaces to enclose fires.
—Clear ground around fireplace so wind cannot blow a spark into leaves, grass, etc.
—Dig a trench in ground if it is windy or there are no stones or logs to enclose fire; pile dirt and sod to one side and replace when through.
—Build small fire.
—Throw used matches into fire.
—Never leave a fire unattended.
—Have some means for fighting fire on hand—pails of water or sand.

6
OUTDOOR FOOD

"When do we eat?" and "What's for lunch?"—these are the big questions that go with any kind of outdoor fun, whether you are hiking for the day, having a picnic in the yard, or cooking for your group at camp. Will it be sandwiches, hamburgers done to a turn, a stew, or reflector biscuits? Outdoor food. It is very important, and the better the food, the better the campcrafting. Many different skills go into outdoor cooking: firebuilding and toolcraft, as well as good planning and preparation. No one can claim to be a good campcrafter who is not a good camp cook.

Outdoor food does not always have to be cooked; a good hike lunch is part of the day when you want to cover lots of ground without taking the time to cook. For backpacking and mountain climbing, lunches are often concentrated, with food that weighs little but is packed full of nourishment.

Outdoor food needs a good bit of planning, packing, preparation, and cleaning up—and that high point, eating. There are all sorts of good things to make, and many different types of cooking to try as you progress along the outdoor cooking trail. Some of these can be for one person, some for the small group, and some for a large crowd. Whatever it is, you will be sure that it will be one of the best parts of the day when someone calls "Come and get it!" and you take that first bite.

Don't be too ambitious to begin with. Start with simple things, and when you have practiced them, progress to something else. Remember that the actual cooking is only a part of the job—making the fireplace, making the fire, and taking care of it will be more than half the job.

Don't think you cannot have a good cookout unless you have steak or ckicken. A good campcrafter can turn out a meal that costs very little, but that is sure to be tasty. In camp or at home, use leftovers and bits of this and that to make something really special. Don't stay at the frankfurter stage, either. Anyone can cook a frankfurter (more or less), and it *is* the great American picnic dish; but you won't be much of a campcrafter if you don't progress to other just-as-good and more-interesting-to-cook things.

Have some pride in how you cook. Anyone can burn a marshmallow, but not everyone knows enough to toast one golden brown. (All right, burn it later if you like charcoal, but no camper will believe you can cook if you always burn the marshmallows or toast.)

In camp you will probably have a chance to talk over plans for cookouts with your tent mates or unit group. Try to cook out often, if it is possible, for you'll learn much campcrafting while you do. In camp it is good to make a trail kitchen near your sleeping quarters, so it is easy to cook any meal.

In town you may have a place in your yard where you and your group can fix up an outdoor fireplace and trail kitchen. Why not?—it will be a wonderful place to learn lots of campcrafting.

Types of Outdoor Food

Here are some of the types of food, cooked or uncooked, that are part of outdoor fun. From your first hike lunch with nothing to cook, through the first steps in cooking, you can progress to the stage where all the parts of a meal are prepared on the trail or where you and your group stage a big meal like a barbecue. If you do not know how to get started, try some things in this order:

—Hike lunches—no cooking, but good planning, good packing;

—Lunches brought by each person, with one thing, like cocoa or soup, cooked for all;

—Something cooked for a group in a large frying pan—like hamburgers or eggs—to go with lunches brought by each person;

—Something cooked by each person in his own small frying pan—like bacon, a hamburger, an egg—to go with lunch brought all prepared;

—Something toasted on a stick—such as sandwiches or frankfurters;

—One-pot meals for a group—(a main dish all in one kettle)—like a stew;

—On-a-stick cooking (other than toasting)— such as bread twists, pioneer drumsticks;

—Reflector-oven baking;

—Tin-can cookery or on-a-rock cookery;

—Aluminum foil cookery;

—Planking—and other types of baking.

Remember that the fire makes the success of the cooking. Learn when to have a quick, hot fire, when to have good coals, when to plan for a fire that burns for a long while. Firebuilding, the making of the fireplace, and cooking go hand in hand.

Hike Lunches

Maybe the first thing you are going to do is to go on a hike with your class or group, with each person bringing his own lunch. A camper will be able to tell at a glance that you are a campcrafter if you've packed a good lunch, plenty of it but not too much—and when you open it, it is still good to eat. Take along the right amount, with an extra mid-afternoon snack, so you do not throw anything away or have anything to carry home.

Sandwiches

Take from two to five sandwiches. Vary the kinds of filling and, if possible, the kinds of bread. Use some dark or enriched bread; for variety make one sandwich with one slice of white and one of dark bread.

For fillings, have one sweet filling (jam), another meat (chopped ham), and a third, vegetable (lettuce). Moist fillings are better than dry. Spread fillings to edges of bread, rather than all in the middle. Buttering both pieces of bread prevents filling from soaking into bread. Some substitutes for sandwiches are:

—A roll stuffed with salad
—A hard-boiled or deviled egg
—A good-sized piece of cheese
—A paper cup of salad (not too moist)
—Crackers, rye crisp (Watch out for fillings that make them soggy.)

Fruit

Take along fresh fruit, especially the kind that will quench thirst—oranges, apples, peaches, pears, tangerines, or grapes.

Include dried fruit such as raisins, prunes, apricots, or figs. A generous handful makes a good portion.

Raw Vegetables

These help to provide moisture and add freshness to the lunch. Carrots, scraped and cut in long strips, celery or radishes are good. Lettuce carries best if washed, dried, wrapped in wax paper, and inserted in the salad or sandwiches on the spot. Tomatoes carried whole, and sliced just before eating, prevent soggy sandwiches. A whole or half tomato to eat, as is, is a fine addition.

Something Sweet

But don't make it *too* sweet. Plain cake, cookies, a chocolate bar, maple sugar, a few nuts, or a few pieces of candy are good choices.

Liquids

Juicy fruit and a not-too-sweet lunch can relieve thirst. A fruit punch is refreshing—you can use the powdered kind with high vitamin content and mix it when you are ready to drink. Instant dry milk is easier to carry and use than fresh milk. Tomato or fruit juices also are good.

As for water—watch out for drinking it "just anywhere"; take it with you if you are not absolutely sure of the supply you may want to use on the hike.

Foods to Avoid

It is wise to avoid foods that:

—will spoil quickly or are perishable;
—are sticky or will get soft in heat, like molasses candy, or chocolate in extreme heat;
—are very rich or soft, like some frostings;
—are apt to get soggy, as pie or crackers with cheese spread;
—do not carry well in pocket or pack, like cream puffs or lemon meringue pie;
—have little food value compared to their size or weight, like canned drinks;
—will taste flat when warm, like canned drinks.

Packing Hike Lunches

When you have decided what to have, give thought to the wrapping and packing. Wax paper, plastic bags, and paper napkins are great boons to hike lunches. A bread wrapper makes a good lunch cover.

Pack lunches in individual plastic bags or in paper bags. These can then be burned after lunch and need not be carried back.

In packing, use plenty of wax paper. Pack heaviest items in bottom. Wedge paper napkins in between them so there is no room for shifting. Prepare vegetables beforehand, and wrap in wax paper or plastic wrap.

There is a variety of light, high protein trail lunches that can be easily packed and carried and will furnish quick energy. Check your local supermarket for high energy breakfast bars, dried fruit, dried trail mixes (fruits, nuts, sunflower seeds), and powdered drink mixes. The natural foods section will have additional quick lunch items. Individual or group portions can be packed in reusable zip-lock bags or small plastic bags secured with twistems. If you want to make your own trail mix, try crunch dry cereal or granola or experiment with your own mix. Some possible ingredients are: peanuts, pecans, sunflower seeds, candy-coated chocolate bits or carob bits (a chocolate substitute), dried dates, small pieces of dried apples, and natural dry cereal toasted in honey.

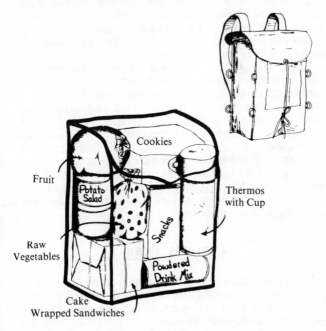

Cookies

Fruit

Potato Salad

Thermos with Cup

Raw Vegetables

Snacks

Powdered Drink Mix

Cake
Wrapped Sandwiches

When You Cook Out

Planning for outdoor meals is very much like that for meals you have at home, as far as the need for them to be good, well-balanced, and attractive. But some things are more fun to cook outdoors. You may plan extra amounts because you'll be hungrier. The fuel you have or the place for cooking may make a difference in what you can plan. If you are just learning, plan only one thing to be cooked, and take along sandwiches, juices, fruit, and ready-made desserts to round out the meal.

Most cooking takes time—time for the water to boil and the food to cook or time for the fire to burn down to coals so your food is not smoked and charred. Plan for a sandwich or some crackers to eat while you wait— you'll do a better job of cooking if the fire is right; you'll like it better if the food is cooked well; and it is easier to wait if you are not *too* hungry.

There are all sorts of good shortcuts for outdoor cooking—mixes, canned, and dehydrated foods. Some canned goods are easier to carry than fresh foods if you are not going too far; concentrated and dehydrated food like soups are good for carrying and good for eating, too. Look in your supermarket for dehydrated soups, convenience foods, sauce and gravy packets, soybean meat substitutes, dried casserole dishes, quick-cooking and dry cereals, and instant drink mixes. If you want to bake, the ready-made mixes are just right. Learn to use Dutch, reflector, or box ovens; they can add the right touch to any meal.

Planning Menus

Simple meals are best. Choose the main item that is to be cooked, and plan the rest of the meal around it. That is, if you have a heavy dessert, plan a light main dish; if you have a good one-pot stew, plan a fruit dessert. To be sure you have a well-balanced meal, follow this plan:

For *one meal*, include:
    an egg, meat, fish, or piece of cheese
    milk, if possible (for drinking and cooking)
    fruit of some kind
    at least one vegetable (except for breakfast)
    dark or enriched bread

In the meals *for a day*, include:
    at least a pint of milk (canned or instant dried)
    fruit of some kind, twice
    cereals or bread, dark or enriched
    two or more vegetables, one of which should be green,
      leafy, or uncooked
    a potato, in addition to another vegetable
    a small portion of meat, cheese, fish, egg, dried
      beans, or peas
    butter or margarine
    something sweet

General Suggestions for Meals

Breakfast:
    fresh or cooked fruit
    hot or cold cereal
    pancakes and bacon or eggs—or
    toast and bacon or eggs—or
    French toast or biscuits
    honey, jam, or syrup as needed
    cocoa or milk

Dinner:
    meat, fish, eggs or cheese
    vegetables, one cooked, one raw
    rice, potatoes, macaroni, noodles or spaghetti
    dessert to balance; fruit with a heavy meal; plan a light
      meal if you want to cook shortcake or doughboys
    milk

Lunch or Supper:
    (Plan this with heavier meal of day in mind; make it
      light if dinner has been or will be heavy.)
    one-pot dishes, salads, and sandwiches, individual stick
      cooking, soups
    raw vegetable or salad
    bread and butter or toast or biscuits
    dessert, as for dinner
    milk or cocoa

As an alternative to cooking three meals a day, you can plan one meal to be a high protein trail lunch or a breakfast of natural cereal which combines honey, nuts, and whole grain cereals with or without milk, or high protein breakfast bars with one of the many brands of liquid instant breakfast.

Types of Outdoor Cooking

If you plan to use a type of cooking which involves any change to the area—cutting green sticks, making pot hooks, digging a trench or hole, be sure that this is permitted in the area where you camp. Select the green sticks or wood to be carved with care so as not to deface the area; if you dig a hole or trench, be sure to follow the practice of cutting and replacing the sod discussed under fire building in Chapter 5.

Here are various types of cooking, and little helps to make them successful.

—*Toasting*—"to brown by heat." This is best done over good coals; patience in waiting for the fire to burn to coals is its own reward. A good campcrafter toasts his bread or marshmallows golden brown, evenly done on all sides. He doesn't say he "likes it burned" just because he is not skillful enough to do a good job.

When a flaming fire must be used, hold the food to one side of the flames, instead of *in* or *over* them, or the food will be smoked instead of toasted.

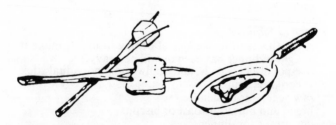

Boiling

Tin Can
Frying

On-A-Rock

—*Broiling*—"to cook by direct exposure to heat." Broiling is a method used in cooking meat, especially tender cuts like chops or steak. It is usually done on a green stick, a wire rack, or broiler.

Broiling is best done over coals; the food should be turned often and cooked slowly. As in toasting, flames will smoke the food.

—*Pan Broiling*—done in a pan (usually for meat). Heat the pan first, put in meat, turn often, pour off fat as it accumulates, keeping pan as dry as possible so meat does not fry.

—*Stewing or Boiling*—"to cook in water." Tougher cuts of meat are good for stew; they have more flavor but take longer to cook. For stews, meat should be browned quickly in fat and then cooked slowly in water until tender. Generally speaking, the longer the cooking, the better the stew.

For boiling, have a cover on the pot to hasten the process; put the kettle on the fire as soon as it is going to catch all the heat.

—*Frying*—"to brown or sear in fat in a pan." Best done over a bed of coals, since flames are likely to lick into the pan. Generally, a small amount of fat is all that is necessary for frying. Draining fried foods on a paper napkin helps to get rid of excess grease.

When frying bacon, onions, etc., for a one-pot meal, fry in the bottom of the kettle to be used and pour off the grease when brown, adding other ingredients as needed.

—*On-a-Rock Cooking*—another kind of frying in which a solid rock (not shale) is heated and used as a frying pan.

—*Steaming*—cooking by steam. Little or no additional moisture is added to the food, so it cooks in its own natural juices. Double boilers are used to cook or warm food. Aluminum foil cooking is also a steam process.

—*Baking*—there are many ways of baking out-of-doors. One way is on the end of a green stick, as you do for a bread twist; this is a slower process than toasting, for the outside must not cook too quickly or the inside will not be cooked.

Another way is in a reflector or box oven. Dutch ovens are also used for baking.

—*Planking*—the art of cooking on a board, generally by reflected heat. It is used for meat and fish.

—*Non-Utensil Meals*—those for which you use no kettles or pans, but make any implements you need, like broilers or toasting sticks. This is a fine campcrafting kind of meal. Your jack-knife is your best friend here.

—*One-Pot Meals*—those where many ingredients make the main dish, like a chowder or stew. Everything is prepared in one kettle and one needs only fruit or sweets to top off the meal.

—*Barbecues*—for roasting large pieces of meat, such as chicken, over coals; a special sauce is used for basting the meat.

Steps in Outdoor Cooking

Suggestions for the simplest things to toast that might be included in lunches:

sandwiches, to be toasted—cheese, meat, jelly, raisin
   bread
bread to be toasted; make the sandwiches on the spot
rolls spread with cheese spread, or just split and toasted
frankfurters
desserts—marshmallows, marguerites,* some-mores,*
   and lots-mores.*

Suggestions for things to cook on a green stick:

foods listed above
steak, bacon or ham, chops, etc.
bread twists*
pioneer drumsticks*
kebabs*
desserts
lots-mores*

Frankfurter in a
Bread Twist

Suggestions for one-pot dishes:

chili con carne*
chowder*
campfire stew*
American chop suey*
savory beans*

Desserts, cooked in a pot:

chocolate drops*
candied apples*

Suggestions for things to bake in a reflector or box oven:

    cookies
    cornflake macaroons
    corn bread
    rolls or biscuits

Suggestions for things to cook in individual, small frying pans or on a vagabond stove or a hot rock:

    anything that can be fried
    hamburgers
    frankfurters
    bacon (better to *start* this way than over an open fire
        on a stick)
    eggs—fried or scrambled
    grilled sandwiches
    pancakes*
    ham or spam slices
    apple and sausages
    hash or fish cakes
    small pieces of meat like cube steak
    scrambled potatoes*

Items that could be baked in the coals:

    potatoes
    potatoes in tin cans*
    fish in a bag*
    roast corn*
    little pig potatoes

On a plank:

    fish
    steak
    chops
    liver

Suggestions for beverages:

bouillon
cocoa*
coffee*
tea

(Recipes of items * starred are at the end of this chapter.)

Using What Is Left Over Or On Hand

Often you can cook out, at home or in camp, without buying special foods.

Chopped meat

fry or broil
pioneer drumsticks*
in almost any one-pot meal that calls for meat*

Frankfurters

broil, boil, or fry
cook in bread twist
cooked—cut in pieces, and used in one-pot dishes, pea soup, or potato salad

Bread or cake mixes
pancakes*
bread twists*
biscuits, corn bread, gingerbread cookies, etc., in a reflector or box oven

Left-over cooked or canned meat or fish

cold sliced
chopped or sliced, in sandwiches

chopped or cubed, in salads
in one-pot dishes or chowders
chopped, in stuffed peppers or hash or meat cakes
chowder*

Dry instant milk

in cocoa or eggnog*
in soups or chowders
in puddings
in pancakes, etc.
anywhere whole milk is used

Rice or spaghetti

as a vegetable instead of potato
in soups and one-pot meals
rice in puddings with raisins or dates as dessert
rice in pancakes or meat cakes

Bacon

broil or fry
cooked—cut in pieces and used in scrambled eggs,
    sandwiches, chowders, one-pot dishes
in club sandwiches, with tomato, toast, etc.

Sugar

fudge
chocolate drops*
candied apples*

Left-over cooked vegetables

Potatoes:
    fry or cream
    with egg, meat, bacon, etc., in salads
    scrambled potatoes*
    mashed

Other vegetables:
    in salads
    in one-pot dishes
    in soups

Eggs
    fried, boiled, scrambled, etc.
    baked in orange skins or potatoes
    hard boiled—in sandwiches, or plain, or stuffed, or in
      salads
    cold scrambled eggs make good sandwich filling
    scrambled potatoes*

A good campcrafter is always making up new recipes—generally because of what is left over.

(Recipes of items * starred are in the recipe section on the pages which follow.)

Basic Recipes

Basic Pancake Recipe

(Serves 8)   (Frying Pan)

3 cups flour
1 tsp. salt
1½ tbsp. baking powder
1 or 2 eggs
2 cups milk
2 tbsp. cooking oil
grease for frying
turners
bowl or pan
spoon
frying pan—individual
   ones are good (or tin
   can stoves

Mix dry ingredients, add eggs then milk, gradually;
last of all oil. Batter should just pour from spoon.

Have the frying pan hot and well greased. Pour spoon-
ful on pan, cook until bubbles appear on top, then turn.
The smaller, the easier for beginners to cook. Try flip-

ping, using individual pans. When using batter for a large group, give each camper a paper cup of batter.

Variation: Add 2 cups blueberries or cooked rice or 2 teaspoons cinnamon and 2 tablespoons sugar.

Bread Twists or Doughboys
(Per person)   (On-a-stick)

½ cup flour
1 tsp. baking powder   (or ¾ cup prepared
1 tsp shortening   biscuit flour)
Pinch of salt
about ¼ cup water
small amount of extra flour
green stick, one end a
   little bigger than thumb;
   peeled 3 inches down
cup or small paper bag
coals

Mix dry ingredients in bag or cup; work in shortening formed. Handle as little as possible to keep dough from getting tough. Make it stiff enough to hold together; add a little flour if it gets too moist. (Only practice will tell you.)

Heat stick; flour it; flour hands; put half mixture on stick, winding like a ribbon spirally down the stick, with space between twists, or place over the end, squeezing gently into a long, thin covering. Cook by holding about six inches away from coals at first so inside will bake, then brown nearer coals. Turn continually. Will slip off stick easily when done. Stuff hole with bacon, jam, or add cinnamon and sugar or butter.

Basic Chowder Recipe
(Per person)   (One-pot)

1 slice bacon
1/8 onion

1/2 medium-sized potato
   (diced)
1/4 can corn
1/4 lb. fish, etc.
salt and pepper
1 cup liquid (water,
   stock or milk)
kettle
jackknife
ladle or spoon

Cut bacon or pork and onions very small. Fry in bottom of kettle until brown. (Stir frequently to prevent burning. Pour off extra grease, if necessary.)

Add corn, fish, or meat, with a little water, as needed. Let cook slowly until fish or meat is cooked. Add diced potatoes about 1/2 hour before time for serving and cook until done. Season and, if using milk, add just before serving. Bring to boiling point, but do no boil.

Cream Sauce

(Serves 8)   (One-pot)

8 tbsps. butter or oleo
8 tbsps. (1/2 cup) flour
1 tsp. salt
4 cups milk
kettle or double boiler
spoon
slow fire

Melt butter (or other fat) in bottom of kettle; add flour, stirring well until smooth paste is formed and mixture bubbles vigorously. Add cold milk, heat, stirring constantly until thick and smooth.

Beginners may use double boiler made by two kettles, one inside the other; put boiling water in outside kettle.

(Some experts say you cannot really cook outdoors until you can make a good cream sauce over an open fire.)

One-Pot Recipes

American Chop Suey

(Serves 8)   (One-pot)

2 cans spaghetti with
    tomato sauce
2 tsps. cooking oil
3-4 onions (small),
    peeled and diced
1-1½ lbs. hamburger steak
green pepper (if desired), cut small
salt and pepper
frying pan or kettle
jackknife

Fry onions and pepper in shortening or oil until brown. Pour off excess. Add hamburger steak and cook until well done, but not crisply brown. Add spaghetti and heat well. Season to taste. Serve hot.

Instead of canned spaghetti, use 1 package macaroni and 1 can concentrated tomato soup. Cook macaroni in boiling water. (Takes an extra kettle.)

For variety: Use a little sausage meat with the hamburger; add some cooked celery or peas.

Scrambled Potatoes

(Serves 8)   (One-pot)

8 medium-sized, cold
   boiled potatoes, diced
2 small onions, peeled
   and diced
4 pieces bacon, cut in
   small pieces, or small
   amount bacon fat
8 eggs
salt and pepper
jackknives
frying pan or kettle

Fry onions with bacon pieces, or in bacon fat until light brown. Add potatoes, and fry until brown and crisp. Break eggs into mixture, stirring while it cooks; cook until eggs are set. Season well. Serve hot.

Add a little cheese or tomato catsup or both, if desired.

Chile Con Carne

(Serves 8)   (One-pot)

4 tbsps. cooking oil
8 tbsps. (about)
   chopped onion
1-1½ to 2 lbs. ground steak
   or left-over meat
2 qts. canned tomatoes
2 cans kidney beans
salt
kettle
spoon
jackknife

Fry onion until light brown. Add meat and cook until done. Add tomatoes and beans and cook together.

Season with a little chili powder and salt. Let it all simmer. Thicken with a little flour if needed. Add 2 tablespoons of Worcestershire sauce, if more seasoning is needed.

Campfire Stew

(Serves 8)   (One-pot)

1-1/2 to 2 lbs. hamburger
  steak
3 tps. cooking oil or
  shortening
1 large onion, peeled and
  diced
2 cans concentrated
  vegetable soup
salt and pepper
kettle or frying pan
jackknife
spoon

Make little balls of hamburger, adding seasoning. Fry with onion in frying pan, or in bottom of kettle, until onion is light brown and balls are well browned all over. Pour off excess. Add vegetable soup and enough water to prevent sticking. Cover and cook slowly until meat balls are cooked all through. (The longer, the better.)

Savory Beans

(Serves 8)   (One-pot)

6 frankfurters or sausages,
  or 1 lb. sausage meat
1 can or 2 cups cooked
  corn kernals
2 cans or 4 cups baked
  beans

1 medium-sized onion,
   peeled and chopped fine
kettle
spoon
jackknife

Cut sausages in small pieces or make small balls of meat, and fry with onion until brown. Pour off any excess.

Add corn and beans. Add a little water, if needed. Season to taste and heat well, stirring to prevent sticking.

Add a little catsup, if desired. Serve hot.

Pocket Stew

(Per person)   (One-pot)

Each person brings a handful of cleaned and diced vegetables, bacon, or meat in bits, and bouillon cubes in a piece of wax paper.

Fry onions and bacon together in pot; add a little water and any meat and vegetables; simmer slowly until done.

Beverages

Cocoa

(Per person)

1 tsp. cocoa
2 tsps. sugar
1 cup milk, or equivalent:
   1/2 cup evaporated
   milk and 1/2 cup
   water; or 4 tbsps. milk
   powder and 1 cup
   water
extra water (a little)
kettle

Mix cocoa and sugar with water in kettle, cook to a smooth paste, letting it bubble vigorously. Add milk and stir thoroughly.

Heat almost to a boil. Some add a pinch of salt. Beating with a whip prevents any scum from forming.

Coffee

(Per person)

1 cup water
1 tbsp. (heaping) coffee
   (regular grind)
1 extra tbsp. coffee for
   every 10 cups (1 lb.
   coffee makes 45 cups)
coffee pot
bag of cheesecloth and
   string

Cold water coffee: Put coffee in bag, place bag in the water in pot, put on fire and bring to a boil. Boil three minutes for ordinary strength, longer for stronger. Remove bag; keep *hot*.

The bag just makes it easier to clean pot. Be sure the bag is large enough to allow coffee to swell. A large square of cheesecloth caught up at the corners does just as well as a bag.

Boiling water coffee: Bring water to a boil, then add the bag of coffee and boil three to four minutes. (Some think this has the advantage of fresher tasting coffee, since coffee has not soaked in water.) Or use instant or freeze-dried coffied in big pot—boil water, add one teaspoon per cup of water and bring to a boil.

Without the bag: Use the same proportions, and clear with egg shells or cold water when cooked.

Non-Utensil Recipes

Fish in a Bag

(Per person)

1/4 to 1/3 lb. solid white
   fish per person (cod,
   haddock or any fillet
   is good)
salt and pepper
lemon butter (3 tbsps.
   melted butter or
   margarine with 1 tbsp.
   lemon juice)
heavy wax paper
newspaper or small
   paper bags
good bed of coals

Place piece of fish in a good-sized piece of wax paper; salt and peptter it, and add lemon butter or piece of butter. Wrap wax paper around fish, turning it on all sides. Then wrap well in bag or newspaper that has been soaked in water.

Have a good bed of coals ready, and place the packet on top of the coals; leave for about 20-30 minutes, depending on size of fish, turning once. If paper becomes too dry, remove from fire and wet again; then return to coals. It cooks by steaming.

Roast Corn

(Per person)

2-3 ears of corn
salt and pepper
butter
string
good bed of coals
grill over coals for
    large number

Peel ears, leaving husks on at bottom, and remove corn silk. Then replace husks, covering ears, and tie around top. (Some people dip corn in salt water at this point.)

Have a good bed of coals in trench or round fireplace, and place screening across logs or stones, just above coals. Place ears on screening. Turn often until all sides are done. Strip ears, leaving husk on the end for a handle; add salt, pepper, and margarine to taste. Eat immediately. May also be done by standing ears upright at sides of fireplace, turning often. If you like the kernels brown, strip ears after they have steamed awhile, and finish cooking by direct exposure to heat, turning as above.

Stick Cookery

Pioneer Drumsticks

(8 persons)

2 lbs. lean, chopped beef
1 cup cornflakes,
   crumbled fine
2 eggs (optional)
pepper, onion, salt,
   if desired
16 rolls or slices of bread
8 green sticks about the
   size of thumb. Peel
   thick end 3 inches
bed of coals

Mix beef, seasonings, eggs, and cornflakes together thoroughly. Make 16 portions.

Wrap a portion around end of a stick, squeezing in place evenly. Make it long and thin, not a ball. Be sure there are no air spaces in it. (Watch out for big pieces of cornflake.) Have a small frying pan to catch the drumstick if it falls.

Cook slowly over coals, turning frequently so all sides are evenly cooked. Twist slightly to take off stick. Serve in roll. Some prefer to roll the meat in crumbled cornflakes after placing it on the stick to make a crust. Try it both ways.

Kebabs

(Per person)

1/4 lb. round steak cut in
   small pieces, trimmed
   of fat, about 1 inch
   square by 1/4 inch thick
small onion peeled and
   cut in slices
partially boiled potato,
   if desired, sliced 1/4 inch
   thick
2 strips bacon, cut in
   squares
2 rolls or sandwiches
pointed green sticks
   about size of little
   finger peeled down
   three inches, or skewers
   made from coat hangers
jackknife
bed of coals

Place pieces of steak, onion, bacon and potato alternately on sticks, pushing them down the stick and leaving a little space between pieces. Repeat in same order.

Sear quickly all over by holding close to coals, then cook slowly a little away from coals, turning until done.

Variations: Oyster Babs—use oysters and pieces of bacon; Liver Babs—use small pieces of liver and pieces of bacon; Pie-Chams—use small pieces of cooked ham and pineapple chunks.

Desserts

Some-Mores

(Serves 8)   (on-a-stick)

16 marshmallows
  (about 1/2 lb.)
32 graham crackers
  (about 1 large pkg.)
6 small, plain chocolate
  bars
green sticks for toasting
  or a skewer made from
  coat hanger

Make a sandwich with a piece of chocolate and two crackers. Toast a marshmallow golden brown and well puffed. (Slowly over coals does it.) Pop into the sandwich; press gently together, and eat. Tastes like "some more."

Variations: Use peanut butter instead of chocolate— "Robinson Crusoes." Use slices of apples instead of crackers—"apple some-mores." Use chocolate-covered

crackers instead of chocolate bars. Use a chocolate pep-
permint instead of milk chocolate.

Marguerites

(Per person)   (On-a-stick)

2 marshmallows
2 soda crackers
2 nut meats (walnuts,
    pecans, or large peanuts)
    green sticks, split on
    thick end, about 3 inches
    down

Place a marshmallow on top of a soda cracker, and a
nut meat on top of the marshmallow. Place all in the
split green stick and toast. Toast cracker side first, then
marshmallow side.

Note: Good way to use stale soda crackers.

Lots-Mores

(Per person)   (On-a-Stick)

3 marshmallows
3 squares milk chocolate
split green stick
jackknife
bed of coals

Split marshmallow through middle. Insert square of
chocolate. Put in split stick and toast. When marshmallow is toasted, chocolate will be melted inside.

Candied Apples

(Serves 8)

1-1/2 lbs. sugar
6 tbsps. butter
1 small can corn syrup
8 good-sized apples
water in cup to test
kettle
pointed sticks about 6
   inches long
spoon
cup

Cook sugar, butter, and syrup in kettle, stirring constantly. When syrup pours heavily from spoon, test in cup of water, cooking until a small amount hardens in water.

Remove from fire, put apple on stick, and dip so that the apple is well coated with syrup. Twirl in air until cool. If syrup seems to harden before all apples are dipped, heat again, or keep kettle in another kettle of hot water while dipping.

Keep hands away from drips—hot.

Chocolate Drops

(Serves 8)

1 cup sugar
1/8 cup cocoa
1/2 cup milk
16-24 marshmallows
small kettle
spoon
small sticks
pieces of wax paper,
   3-inch squares
cup of water

Make a fudge of sugar, cocoa, and milk, stirring enough to keep from sticking. When fudge is cooked enough to make a soft ball in a cup of water, remove from fire. Place marshmallows on stick and dip into fudge, turning until well covered, but not too long. Twist in air, using wax paper squares to catch the drips. Eat when cool. The second round will be cooler, and will form a hard coating of fudge on the marshmallow.

Variation: Make brown sugar fudge.

Trail Foods

Crunch Dry Cereal

3 cups rolled oats
1 cup wheat germ
1 cup sesame seeds or
   sunflower seeds
1 cup shredded,
   unsweetened coconut
1/4 cup oil
3/4 cup honey
1 tsp. vanilla
dash of salt

Mix all ingredients. Spread 1/2-inch deep on cookie pan and bake at 250 degrees until golden brown. Stir occasionally as the sides will brown first. Let cool. Good for breakfast with milk, or for trail lunch.

Granola

4 cups rolled oats
1 cup wheat germ
   cup sunflower seeds

1 cup roasted soybeans
    (chopped)
3/4 cup coconut
1/2 cup sesame seeds
1 cup chopped nuts
1/2 cup oil
3/4 cup honey
1-1/2 tsp. vanilla

Mix the dry ingredients in a large bowl. Heat oil, honey, and vanilla until combined. Pour mixture over dry ingredients and mix well. Spread on oiled cookie sheet. Bake at 350 degrees for 20 to 30 minutes or until lightly browned. Stir frequently. Add 1 to 2 cups of raisins when cool. Makes 3 pounds. Good with milk for trail lunch or for snack.

High Protein Lunch

1/4 cup raisins (about 25)
4 squares rye crackers
4 ounces cheese
4 ounces hard salami
4 ounces of chocolate
peanut butter
punch made from
    powdered mix

Baking

Potatoes Baked in Tin Can

(Serves 8)

8 medium-sized potatoes
2 #10 cans, with wire
   handles (punch holes
   on opposite sides of
   can near top to insert
   wire handle)
heavy wax paper
sand or dirt
good bed of coals

Scrub potatoes well and wrap each in wax paper. Put a layer of sand or dirt in bottom of a can; then put in potatoes with sand or dirt in between so no potato touches another potato or sides of the can. Pack sand or dirt well around the potatoes, and cover well. Wet the sand or dirt until a bit of it holds its shape when squeezed.

Have a good, hot bed of coals ready, and place the cans directly in the coals, piling coals around the sides. Leave for about an hour, keeping coals raked around the cans. (Time varies a little with size of potatoes. When the ones on top are done, they are all done.) Moisten sand occasionally if it becomes too dry, adding water with a cup.

For Baking with Reflector or Box Oven

Beginners should try small objects like cookies, rather than whole cakes. Try any cookie, gingerbread, or cake recipe or a ready-packed mix and make cinnamon rolls or prepared biscuits.

Marguerites (see recipes) also are good in a reflector oven.

Another type of baking can be done in a Dutch oven.

Camp Cooking Helps

Broilers and sticks for toasting may be fashioned as shown from green sticks—if you are in areas where cutting of limbs and small sticks is permitted. If you cut

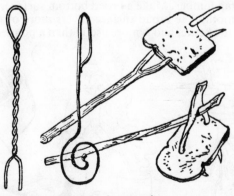

Broilers and sticks for toasting

natural materials, select them with care so that the pruning you have done will not show. Cut throughout a large area rather than getting the materials from one spot.

Other cooking tools may be made by twisting wire or coat hangers into the shape desired. If the hangers are painted or coated, remove the covering with sand paper before forming the wire into cooking utensils.

A Cooking Paddle

Make a wooden paddle for stirring stews, cocoa, or soup. Make it long enough to extend outside your largest kettle, or make several sizes. It can be made from scrap lumber. Make a broad bottom surface, sandpaper smooth. The broad surface covers more of the bottom of the kettle, and is more useful than a pointed spoon.

Other Helps

A whip from a green twig; a bandana for a pot holder or a handy towel on your belt; a "table" near the fireplace for spoon or paddle; smear liquid or bar soap on the outside of kettles—for easier cleaning.

Wind

Fix your trench fireplace so that your kettles or pans rest securely without someone having to hold them. Cook with the wind at your back. Put kettle on as soon as you start the fire.

A round fireplace is good for a Dutch oven or when several people are toasting or broiling at the same time.

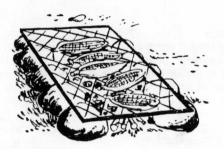

Roasting on a Grill

Wire over coals is good for roasting corn, potatoes, or foil packets.

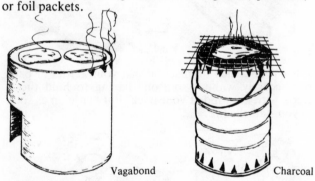

Vagabond

Charcoal

Cut door; punch holes in opposite sides for draft; heat top grease and wipe off; then grease again and fry on top.

Frying on a Vagabond Stove

A vagabond stove conserves fuel. It may be made from #10 cans, or from larger cracker or shortening tins. To fry on top of stove, grease the top, heat, and then wipe clean when the stove is cool. Grease the top again before frying on it.

Aluminum Foil Cookery

Aluminum foil cookery is a simple way to cook outdoors. The secret of good foil cookery is used using duty foil and adding liquid to the food and sealing the foil properly so that juices do not escape and leave food dry and burned. You need a fire of coals. Wrap the food carefully in the foil, with all seasoning inside; turn edges so that no steam can escape, folding over twice at each edge, and leaving air space inside. For example—a hamburger patty with onions, celery, carrot, tomato catsup—all wrapped together. Place this on top of coals or on a grill over coals and leave for five to ten minutes turning at least once, depending on what is inside. Here is one method of folding the foil for best results.

The disadvantage of aluminum foil is that it cannot be easily disposed of. If you are hiking or camping in an area where garbage containers are not accessible, you should be prepared to take the used foil out of the area with you. Aluminum foil is easy to transport and use, but it is expensive.

Cook Kits

Perhaps you have a cook kit that has a frying pan, small kettle, plate, cup, and so forth, with its own cover. This is a good start in the way of having your own equipment. Make one, if you do not have one; a small frying pan, an enamel or plastic plate and cup, and a tin can kettle make a fine kit.

One of the best things is a kettle with a bail or handle—a nest of such kettles is even better. A nest of cooking kettles can be made from tin cans and coat hangers. A #10 can, a #5 can, and a #3 can will make a set of nested kettles—or use a set of coffee cans: 3-pound, 2-pound, or 1-pound. Larger kettles can be made with commercial cracker tins or any large, round tin. Make a handle out of a coat hanger and insert in holes drilled in the sides of the can across from each other. Be sure to remove any paint or coating from the coat hangers so that the paint will not flake or drop into the kettle. Season your cans before cooking with them by heating and then allowing to cool—if the outside of the can has paint that begins to flake off, use steel wool or sandpaper to remove it.

If you prefer, you may buy a set of nested kettles in aluminum or stainless steel at many camping equipment stores.

Packing Foods

Pack baskets, knapsacks, or kettles are generally used to carry food for outdoor meals. Kettles with handles on them can easily be used as containers.

Pack heaviest things in the bottom of baskets or kettles. Pack so that there is no room for the various articles to shift around.

Wrap eggs in paper napkins, or carry them in an egg carton, or put them in the bag of flour to carry them safely.

Waterproofed cotton bags are excellent for carrying dry food. A good campcrafter will make his own.

7
KNOT CRAFT

Ever break a shoestring? Ever wanted to put up a line for drying your wet clothes? Ever tried to tie up a blanket roll? Ever tried to hitch a boat or a horse? You needed a knot—and the right one. Knots are an important part of a campcrafter's equipment, and with a good rope in his knapsack and the know-how in his head and fingers, a campcrafter will find knots as useful in camp as a sailor does on a ship. Besides, many skills and crafts that are based on knot tying (also called macrame) provide leisure time fun.

There are hundreds of knots, each made just so, each for a specific use. Learn a few to begin with, and others will be easy to learn. The history of knots and the story of rope-making are both fascinating. Many books about ropes and knot tying will give you more than the glimpse given here.

Knot tying is a general term used for the making of bends, hitches, knots, slings, splices, and lashings—all methods of tying rope or cord. Certain knots are used for certain purposes; there are several types of knots, and it is important to learn why you tie a certain knot while you are learning to tie it. Here are some types:

—Knots used for *joining* ropes or cord or string,
—*Stopper* or *end* knots, to keep ropes from slipping
—through a hole or ring, or to keep the end from ra-
—veling,
—*Loop* knots, providing a loop in the rope,
—Hitches for *securing* rope, to make "fast,"
—Knots for *shortening* rope, and
—Slings for *holding* articles.

A good knot is one that can be tied easily, will hold fast, will not jam, and can be untied easily. Your own invention of several knots one on top of another may hold, but it probably does not qualify for the last test of a good knot. A thrifty camper does not cut a good piece of rope; he uses a knot, and later uses the rope again.

Start by learning one knot of each type, and you will have a good set of knot tricks in your campcraft knapsack. Here's how to start:

1. Get a piece of old clothesline or small rope, such as venetian blind or drapery rod cord, about four feet long.
2. Look at the pictures, and follow step-by-step—or get someone who knows how to teach you.
3. When you can tie from the pictures, try the knot out on a chair, a tree, a box, or however it is supposed to be used.
4. Try to catch the feel of the knot—learn how it looks when it is right.
5. Practice—and practice. Do it with your eyes shut, or behind your back.
6. Find ways in your everyday life to use knots—there are lots of times when just the right knot helps the situation.

Whipping a Rope

When the end of the rope keeps fraying, a way to stop it is to whip it. This makes it look better, keeps the rope intact, and makes it easier to handle.

The simplest ways to stop raveling temporarily are:

1. Wrap a small strip of plastic or cloth tape around the end, or
2. Tie a small piece of string tightly around the end, or
3. Make an overhand knot, if the rope is small.
4. For nylon rope, heat the end with a match until it melts slightly.

But the campcraft way to do it for a permanent end is to whip it. You will need your rope and a piece of string about twelve inches long.

Make a loop of one to two inches with one end of the string (a) and place it on the end of rope so that it lies along the rope. The short end of string (b) and the long end (c) should hang off the rope's end. Hold loop of string on rope with one thumb and fore-finger, so loop a is on top of rope, and ends hangs off end (Fig. 1).

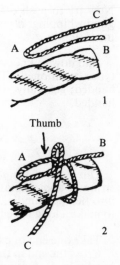

Holding thumb near end of rope, start winding string (c) *back down the length of rope*, away from the end, being sure to leave the short end (b) hanging off the end of the rope (Fig. 2).

As you wind neatly and tightly away from end, be sure to catch the string under your winding, letting your thumb slip back as you secure it, winding toward loop a, but not covering it.

When you have wound about 3/4 of an inch, stop winding and tuck the end (c) with which you have been winding, into the loop (a) and pull (c) taut (Fig. 3).

The short end of string (b) should be still hanging off the end of the rope. Now pull this end (b), and you will discover that the loop (a) with the other end of cord (c) is slowly disappearing under the winding. Pull until you figure that the loop is about halfway down under the winding (Fig. 4), and then cut off both ends of string close to winding.

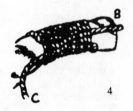

Now try to push off the whipping. If you can't, it is a good whipping; if you can, try again, winding the string more tightly.

And now to knots—here are just a few of some of the types mentioned. The methods described are right-handed; generally you can reverse them if you are left-handed.

Square Knot

This is used for *joining* two ends of rope, cord, or string of approximately the same size or thickness. Use it to tie up a bundle, a bandage, a broken shoelace, or to make a long rope from several short ones.

Take one end of each rope, one in either hand.

Cross the end in the right hand over the end in the left hand (Fig. 1), twisting it back and down then up in front, so that you make a single knot, and the end you started with is now in your left hand (Fig. 2).

Now take the end that is in your right hand and bend it over to the left so that it makes a loop and lies along the knot already made (Fig. 3).

Look closely and you will see that there is only one place for the other end (now in your left hand) to go, and that is into the loop you have made (Fig. 4).

Take hold of the long ends of the rope on both sides, and tighten by pulling them in opposite directions (Fig. 4). To loosen the knot, take hold of the ends on both sides, and push toward the center of the knot (Fig. 5).

Look at the knot: Does it look square? Each piece of rope should double back and lie alongside of itself, going in and coming out.

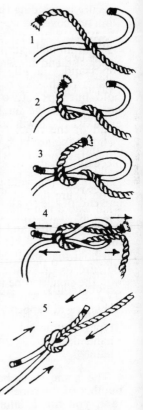

Beware of a granny knot—made by someone who does not know how to tie a square knot. It is a square knot gone wrong—will not hold, looks wrong, pulls loose—try it.

You will notice that the square knot is for joining ropes of the same thickness. What about two ropes of different sizes? The sheet bend works in this case; it is the square knot with an extra twist in it, making sure it will hold fast.

Sheet Bend

Make a square knot in the ends of the two ropes (Fig. 1). Pull the ropes and you will see that the smaller of the two ropes will not hold, but slips out, so the thing to do is to give the smaller rope an extra twist so it will hold.

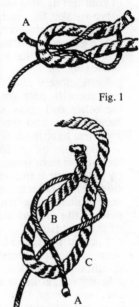

Fig. 1

Fig. 2

Take the end of the smaller rope (a) and cross it under the other piece of the same rope at (b), and then up and over the loop of the bigger rope at (c). This will make one end of the small rope on top and one underneath the loop of the bigger rope; and as you pull the knot tight, this extra turn will hold that small end in place. Be sure to make the extra twist with the smaller rope (Fig. 2). But try it the other way if you want to see what will happen.)

The name sheet bend comes from sailing days—a number of the ropes used to rig a ship are called sheets (and you are a landlubber if you call them ropes). Bending is a way of making a loop.

There are a number of ways to make a sheet bend; the one shown here is used in joining the ends of two ropes. The weaver's knot is a sheet bend tied by weavers using a special method.

Bowline

This knot is used when you need a loop in the end of a rope. Its special feature is that the loop will not pull tight, but will remain the size you make it. Use it to slip over a peg or hook, or make the loop *around* a post or pole.

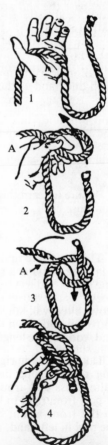

Work with just one end of the rope; the other end may be tied to something else, or may be a coil or long length of rope.

Judge how big a loop you want, and place left hand at about the place you want the knot. Let the rope lie across the palm of your left hand (Fig. 1).

With the right hand, make a loop up and back of the fingers of the left hand, coming down in front, and catching the rope with the left thumb as it crosses over a (Fig. 2).

Let the fingers slip out of the loop, and take the end of the rope in the right hand, holding it at point (a) with left thumb and finger. Pass the end of rope up from underneath into the small loop (Fig. 3).

Pull this end to make the main loop of knot the size you will want it, and then pass the end in back of the standing part of rope and back to the front and down into the small loop again so that it lies beside itself (Fig. 4).

Take these two pieces of rope in one hand and the main part of the rope in the other, and pull in opposite directions to pull knot tight (Fig. 5).

If you want that loop to be around something, as around a bar, pass the end around the bar before you put it through the small loop; pull it as tight as you want it, then proceed as above (Fig. 6).

Sailors learn to make this knot with one hand as they hold on to the rigging with the other. Perhaps you will want to progress to that.

Be sure to learn this knot with just *one* end of the rope; don't use both.

Clove Hitch

This is used to make fast an end of rope, as in starting a lashing or tying a rope to a post. Avoid using it when one end is tied to something that moves, like a boat or a horse, as the movement will tend to loosen the knot. A clove hitch will stay in place when tight, and will not move up and down the post. Do this knot with just one end, too; let the length of rope hang down.

Take one end in right hand, letting rest of rope lie across left palm. Pass end around the back of post from right to left and back to the front again; cross it over the part in left hand, making an X

(Fig. 1). Hold that X loosely away from the post, with thumb on top, index finger under the X, pointing to the right.

Make another turn around the post, from right to left, this time lower than the first turn, bringing end around and under the X, between the two turns, so that the end points to the right (or in same direction finger points), and the long piece of rope leads off left (Fig. 2).

Pull these ropes in opposite directions (Fig. 3).

You will want to pull the long end directly from the center of the knot; to do so may require moving knot around the post. To do this, loosen knot by pushing both ends of the rope toward the center of the knot at X. Then swing knot around until it is in desired position (Fig. 4).

To make a clove hitch on a horizontal bar, follow the same general directions, starting by passing the end over, and in back, of bar (Figs. 5-6).

If you want to be able to undo this knot quickly, double the short end, and slip under loop at X, instead of pulling through (Fig. 7). Pull end (b) to tighten. To untie, pull end (a) (Fig. 8).

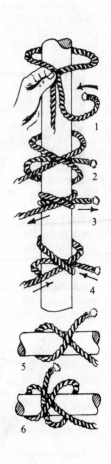

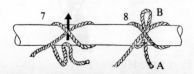

You may find someone to show you how to make this knot slip over the top of a post—it's easy. But you can't use this method on a tree.

Here are three more—easy to make, and very useful:

—Two Half Hitches. Use to make rope fast to a ring or a post. One half hitch is often used to give extra holding power to a knot.

—Overhand Knot. Use to keep end from raveling, or as a "stopper" at any place in rope.

—Taut Line Hitch. Use to fasten tent rope to stake.

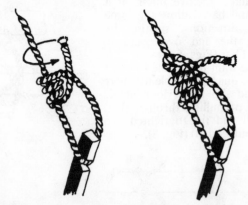

Taut Line Hitch

Ways to Use Knots in Camp

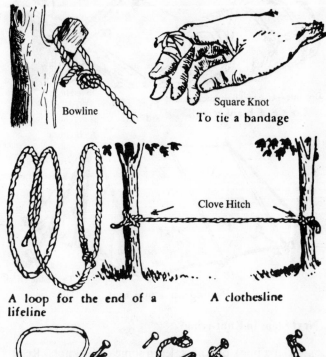

Bowline

Square Knot
To tie a bandage

Clove Hitch

A loop for the end of a lifeline

A clothesline

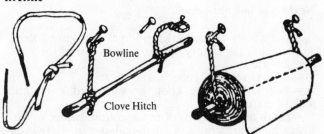

Bowline

Clove Hitch

Square Knot
To mend a shoe lace

A holder for paper

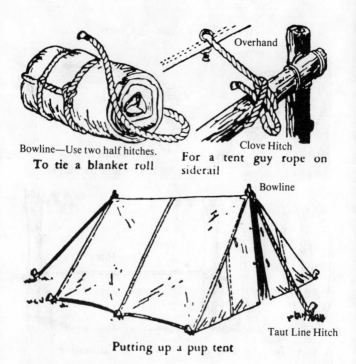

Bowline—Use two half hitches.

To tie a blanket roll

Overhand

Clove Hitch

For a tent guy rope on siderail

Bowline

Taut Line Hitch

Putting up a pup tent

Next Steps in Knot-tying:

—Get a book on knots; learn some other knots. Read a little about the history of knots, and some of the ways they are used.

—Learn to splice a rope.

—Learn the netting knot, or a lanyard knot, and make a craft article.

—Learn different types of ropes: cotton, hemp, nylon. Visit a hardware store and ask the salesperson to tell you about ropes.

8
LASHING

When you need a camp table, a coat hanger, or a basin rack or some fixin's and furnishin's for your campsite, you will be glad that you know lashing. It is a sign of a good campcrafter to be able to make something out of the materials you find around you—and to have them fit into the woodland surroundings.

Lashing is a method of fastening sticks, or dowels, or broom handles together by binding with cord—not with nails. So, it is good to use on living trees; is easily taken apart, and is good for a temporary structure. It is rustic looking, so it fits into camp and requires few tools in the making. A good lashing is neat and attractive and holds securely.

A *square* lashing joins two sticks together at right angles.

A *diagonal* lashing joins two sticks in the form of an X or on the diagonal, preventing scissor-like movement.

A *sheer* or *round* lashing joins two sticks along the length of one, rather than at an angle.

A *continuous* lashing holds several small sticks at right angles to a long stick.

The materials used depend on the size of the article to be made, its intended use, and, to some extent, on what is handy. Strings and twigs can be used in making small craft articles like picture frames, while heavy cord, strong saplings, and large dowels or broomsticks should be used for articles like tables or seats. Binder twine, a shaggy kind of cord available at most hardware stores, is often used because it is inexpensive and very tough.

A finer cord or string can be used to give a more finished effect.

Knot-tying is the starting point of all lashing; the clove hitch, the half hitch, and the square knot should be learned before starting lashing. (See chapter 7.)

Here's how to learn:

1. Get three sticks or dowels about as thick as your thumb, and twelve inches long (the straighter and smoother, the better).
2. Have a piece of cord about thirty-six inches long.
3. Start with square lashing. Get someone to help you if you can, or figure it out from the pictures—the other types will be easy.
4. When you have done the lashing once, take it out and try several times before finishing it off.
5. Look it over—get the feel of it.
6. Make something simple like a coat hanger or a towel rack.
7. Get a group of friends to help make something like a camp table.

Square Lashing

Place sticks in position (Fig. 1). Tie clove hitch to vertical stick at one end of cord, slipping knot around so that the long length of the cord pulls directly out from the knot. Be sure you do not pull back *against* the knot, but pull so that you tighten the knot.

Bind sticks together by passing the cord down in front of horizontal stick, under, out to back of upright, around upright and out to front, (*under* the horizontal stick) then up, in front of horizontal stick, in back of upright, and cord is at starting point (Fig. 2). Repeat this winding several times, following the first turns, and pulling tightly, as you make the cord lie neatly beside previous turns. Be sure to follow the "square" you have made, and do not cross the cord over the center of the sticks, either on the top or underneath (Fig. 3 and 4).

When the sticks are firmly bound, tighten the binding with a *frapping*. This is done by winding the cord *between* the two sticks, so the first binding is pulled together more tightly (Fig. 5).

End by making two half hitches around one stick, or by joining the end of binding cord to the starting end by a square knot. Clip off, and tuck the ends underneath the lashing.

Diagonal Lashing

Place sticks in position, forming and X, and hold them in this position continually (Fig. 6).

Make a clove hitch around the two sticks, as shown (Fig. 6). Make three or four turns around one fork (Fig.

7), then three or four turns around the other fork, pulling tightly (Fig. 8).

Frap and end as in a square lashing.

Sheer or Round Lashing

Place sticks in desired position.

Start with a clove hitch around one stick. Take several turns around both sticks, making sure the turns lie tightly and neatly beside each other (Fig. 9).

Frap, and end with two half hitches or by joining ends with a square knot, tucking both ends under the lashing.

Continuous Lashing

Have sticks cut and ready, long ones the desired length, short ones the size desired for the width of the finished article, and approximately all the same diameter. Mark or notch the long sticks at even intervals where the small sticks will be lashed to make the small sticks fit into place (Fig. 10).

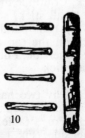

Take a cord approximately four times longer than the long stick. (This will vary with the size of the sticks and the cord.)

Start with a clove hitch at one end of the long stick at the *middle of the cord*, so there are equal lengths on either side of the long stick. Place this hitch so that the ends of the cord pull the knot tight as they come up from the underside of the long stick (Fig. 11).

Bringing the cords around from this knot, pull them over the first small stick following the lines of the long stick (Fig. 12). Pull down and under, crossing the cord on the underside of the long stick (Fig. 12), and coming up again, ready to bind the second small stick. Pull cords over the second small stick in the same manner, following the lines of the long stick, going under, crossing underneath the long stick, and coming up ready for the third stick. Continue this to the end of the small sticks so that the cord always runs parallel to the long stick on the top and crosses on the underside. Pull tightly at each small stick.

End by two half hitches, and tuck ends of cord under last small stick. For a table, repeat on the other side. (Fig. 13)

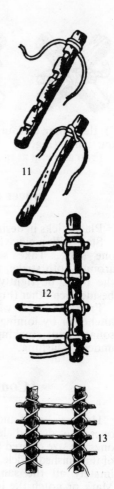

A Few Things to Lash

Coat Hanger

Select two sticks, as illustrated, one with a natural fork, and the other very smooth and slightly curved. Trim ends smoothly. For best results, notch at joining point. Use square lashing.

Picture or Mirror Frame

Select four smooth twigs or branches. Trim neatly, making them the desired size. Notch at joining points. Use square lashings, binding with string or fine cord for small frames.

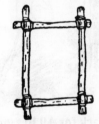

Use the same lashing for a suitcase rack, to raise suitcase off the damp ground, or to prevent scraping on floor.

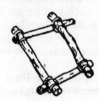

Or make a shoe rack, to facilitate sweeping floor and to keep the tent tidy. Raise in back by small pegs.

Peg for Pole or Tree

Select forked stick, trim neatly and flatten on back, as needed, to fit closely to pole or tree. Use sheer lashing. You may need two lashings.

A Rack for All Reasons

A rack can be used for hanging towels, swimsuits, or for keeping lunches, sweaters, etc., off ground on day hikes. Use square lashings. Look for two convenient trees, or make a set of tripods with diagonal lashings.

A Tripod Basin Rack

Select three sturdy sticks of about the same thickness. Trim to same length, and smooth off rough spots. Leave forks that may be utilized for hanging up items such as wash cloths. Point at ends if the rack is to be used outdoors.

Hold with hand, and spread apart to judge height wanted. Try a basin on the top, and mark place for lashing which will bring basin to right height.

Lash all three sticks together in a sheer type lashing, then spread evenly in a tripod, and bind as in a diagonal, lashing two ways to hold in place.

Drive points in ground, or strengthen if necessary by bracing at the sides (square or diagonal lashing).

Another way to make a tripod is to bind all three sticks together and then twist the middle pole until the lashing is tight. Spread as above. One twist will probably do it.

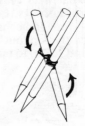

Braces for Tables, Woodpiles, Etc.

Use diagonal lashings.

A Table Top for the Kitchen or a Seat. Cut and trim all pieces as needed. Two convenient trees are a big help, or you will need four sturdy posts and possibly braces on side. The two side sticks must be strong, and as straight as possible. Notch the places for the smaller cross sticks for better results. Lash these in place with square lashing first.

Use continuous lashing for top.

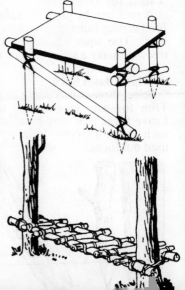

Go on from Here

When you know the steps in the four types of lashing, begin to take pride in well-trimmed ends (good use for your sharp jackknife).

Use dowels or broom handles, in town or where dry branches are not available.

It is not necessary to cut green sticks, but if you do, learn what trees grow the best, straightest, smoothest sticks for lashings. Learn what to cut, how to cut, and where—for good conservation.

Be on the lookout for odd shapes of branches, good forks and so on, to make more interesting articles.

9
TOOLCRAFT

When you need a stick for cooking or shavings to start a fire, or when you want to just sit around and whittle, your knife is on call. You may own a jackknife or a sheath knife; if you do, you'll know that it is your most useful campcrafting tool. To do good campcrafting, you will need one—one you keep for your own use, one you keep in good working condition.

You will use other tools in camping, too, and an axe will come next, either a hand axe or a lightweight, long-handled axe to use with both hands. (No two people agree on which is better to start with; you will have to decide for yourself.)

Using any sharp-edged implement means responsibility—responsibility for your own safety and the safety of other people. A campcrafter learns to use tools safely, knows how to take care of them, and knows how to keep them in good working condition. He does not need to apologize because his knife will not cut or because his axe has a large nick in it. A good campcrafter has respect for property, too; he does not just play with his knife for something to do. A campcrafter respects living things, and he takes what he needs and no more; he appreciates the beauty of wood, and he leaves it as he finds it on buildings or fences.

Here are things you will want to know about any tool:

1. Know *what* it is for—know each part of it.
2. Know how to oil, clean, sharpen, or whatever is necessary to do to put it in good shape and keep it so.
3. Know how to handle it skillfully.
4. Know the precautions for using it safely.
5. Know what to do with it when not in use.
6. Practice—make things with it; practice some more.

There is an old saying that a good craftsman is known by his tools; a good campcrafter is known, too, by the way he handles them and takes care of them.

Knives

There are a number of different kinds of knives. See how many you and your friends or fellow campers can gather, and look them all over. Most common are jack-knives, and sheath or hunting knives. Jackknives fold, so the blade is carried inside the handle; sheath knives are straight, do not fold, and generally have a leather sheath in which they are carried.

Some Types of Knives:

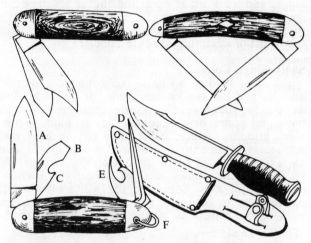

Two-bladed knife; small-bladed knife for whittling; four-bladed knife with (a) blade, (b) screwdriver, (c) bottle opener, (d) awl, (e) can opener, (f) ring for belt; sheath knife (not a jackknife; blade does not fold into handle).

Cleaning and Oiling a Knife:

Don't

For a jackknife, put a drop of machine oil on the hinge, and work blade open and shut a few times; it should work easily. For any knife: clean blade with drop of oil and piece of tissue, cloth, and steel wool. Do not rub in dirt or sand; this may chip blade.

Sharpening a Knife

Use some kind of a sharpening stone; your mother may let you use her kitchen stone, or you may find another for your own. Sharpening stones are known as hones, oil stones, or whetstones. They are made to provide a grinding surface, and come in varying degrees of coarseness. Coarse stones are used for heavy tools, like axes; fine stones for knives or for finishing an edge. Oil or water is sometimes used to reduce the friction, especially for axes. Sometime you will want a small pocket stone to keep with you all the time so you can work on your knife or axe anytime you are sitting around.

Hold the stone with thumb and forefinger *below* the top edge. Hold knife blade flat on stone. Move with a circular motion, with pressure away from the knife edge. Turn the blade and repeat circular motion on other side.

Keep this up at least three times longer than you think is necessary. To test the edge, try it on a piece of wood, not your finger. Try to get a long thin edge that spreads evenly back to the thickest part of blade; the marks of the stone should show all across the blade. (There are many ways to sharpen a knife; get some experienced person to show you his way; then figure out the way you think is best.)

If there is a nick in the blade, use a coarse stone and tip the blade at any angle. Wear away enough of the edge of blade along its length to make an even edge. Finish off with a fine stone.

Using a Jackknife

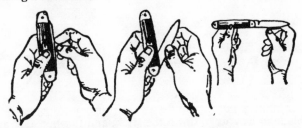

Hold knife in both hands, right thumbnail in slot; pull blade out; keep hold with both hands until open.

To Close: Reverse above, holding blade until it is nearly closed, then letting it snap shut. Avoid closing with *one* hand. Keep fingers in *back* of edge. (Except for opening and closing, the sheath knife is used in the same way.)

Using a Knife

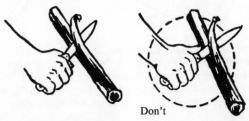

Don't

Take a firm grasp on the handle. Push with your whole hand, not with your thumb. (You don't get the same push.)

Whittle away from you (until you are an expert). Be sure that nothing (your leg, another camper, a branch) is in the way of the sweep your knife will take if it slips. Move your hand over the arc the knife might cover, just to be sure.

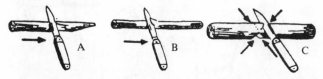

To make a point, whittle away from you, digging the blade in as you go down the stick, and turning stick as you cut, to make an even point (a). To cut across a stick, cut on the diagonal (b). For a large stick, or to make a notch—cut diagonally on one side, then on opposite side to make a V. Slant cut; don't try to cut straight across (c).

To make shavings, try to get long, thin pieces, not little, scrubby bits. Dig the blade into the wood a bit, and start on a piece of wood without many knots (d).

To trim a branch, cut away from the thick end toward the top of branch. Start at bottom and trim down the branch (e).

Cut close to the ground, leaving a smooth cut, not a jagged edge.

When cutting a green stick, get it from a thicket where it will not be missed. Look for one with the kind of fork you will need. Avoid cutting on the edge of a path or road.

When Knife Is Not in Use

Usually it is best to close it before putting it down. When you put it aside for a minute, be sure to place it on its *side*, not on its back with the blade up (think what might happen) and not stuck in the dirt or sand.

Don't

Passing an Open Knife

The person handing should hold the knife by the blade, passing the handle to the other person. In this way the hander has control of the edge of the knife.

The best way to test your knife for sharpness and your hand for skill is to try the knife out on a piece of wood. Start with a piece of kindling wood or a piece of a box end. Make some shavings, or whittle it down to make a round peg. You will progress to rough sticks from the woods. Can you sharpen a pencil easily, with a good point? That's a good test, too.

When you have made some of the articles shown later in this chapter, you will want to progress to fancy whittling—balls in boxes, or chain, or woodcarving.

Using a Hand Axe

A hand axe is a small axe usually used in one hand. Its flat head can be used as a hammer. It is a handy tool for general use, though for heavy chopping a two-handed axe is necessary. The hand axe presents most of the problems of the two-handed axe and can be just as dangerous when carelessly used.

When not in use: Do not leave it in a tree. Do not leave it *on* or *in* the ground.

Hang it on two nails, or leave in a chopping block, or keep sheathed, wear on belt, or carry with blade down.

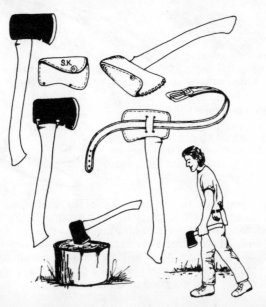

Sharpening a Hand Axe

Hold the axe in left hand by the head; hold sharpening stone in right. Use a rather coarse stone. Work stone on the axe blade. Finish with fine stone. Use a little water on stone to reduce friction.

Hold axe by head. Move stone in circular motion against the edge, keeping it flat on blade. Turn axe, and repeat.

Using a Hand Axe

Do not grasp near head of axe. Grasp end of handle firmly, thumb around fingers. Raise by arm and wrist motion, letting the weight of head of axe help to bring it down in place. Sharp, firm blows make for better progress than pecking, ineffectual, quick blows. Take plenty of time. Be sure to stand and hold axe so that if axe glances or misses, it will not strike your leg or any other part of your body.

Right

Wrong

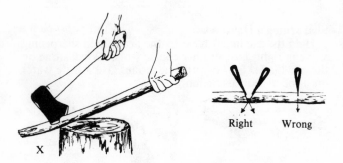

X

To cut across a stick, strike on edge of block (X); hold at least two feet away from the point you will strike. Make diagonal cuts. Don't try to cut square across a stick.

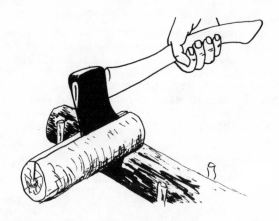

To point a stick, hold at angle on chopping block. Strike at angle, turning to make a point.

To split a log, place the axe on stick; raise both together and bring down, striking on edge of block. Repeat if necessary. Lay the stick flat on block. Do not hold. Raise axe, and bring down sharply in center of stick. Or lean the stick against a log and strike in center of stick where it touches the log. The flat part of an axe is a good hammer.

When passing an axe to someone else, the handle goes first.

You may see experts holding a small piece of wood on end to split it; wait until you are an expert to try it—it pays to be safe.

A good test of axemanship is to be able to split a three-inch log into small kindling. Practice making kindling from box ends first.

Using a Two-Handed Axe

Start with a light axe, a "boy's" size, or one with a 1/2 lb. head and a handle about 24 inches long. Do not try to learn to use an axe alone—get someone to help you, and to be with you when you first begin to chop.

Try first on a small log that is on the ground; put pegs in at four points to keep it steady if it is not heavy enough to stay still.

1. Hold axe easily in both hands, right hand with palm *under* handle at the head, left with palm *over* at end (or reverse if you are left-handed).
2. Stand facing log, feet apart, so weight is even and easy—just far enough away from log to reach it with your arms outstretched and the axe on the log.

3. Be sure there are no branches or anything overhead or in front or to the side in the arc your axe will swing. Try it to be sure.
4. Practice the swing a few times, just letting the axe fall on log without trying to cut anything—like this:

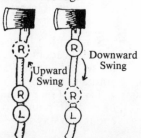

Count one, two—three, and try to get a good, easy, even swing, with no stops between counts.

Count 1—Raise axe head with right hand (at the head) just in front and over your head. Left hand moves up and a little to front—not much. Elbows bent.

Count 2—Let right hand slip down handle to other hand as head of axe falls, with right hand guiding the handle. Keep your eyes on the spot you want to hit.

Count 3—As the axe falls (let the weight do the work), straighten elbows (not stiff), and guide the axe so it bites into the log.

5. As you get the swing, you will find that you put pressure on at points two and three to hit harder. The end of the axe (left hand) will not move very much—the head does the swinging.

Safety Note: Your feet are apart with your weight distributed evenly so that the axe will slip between your legs if it misses the log. Your eyes must be always on the spot you want to hit. If you look at your foot when the axe is coming down, you are likely to hit that foot.

You will be good when you can chop through a five-inch log—easily, and without too many strokes. But it takes a good axe, patience, and plenty of practice. Do not do it alone.

When you are good at this, get someone to help you cut down a small tree. (Practice good conservation in choosing the tree.)

Bow Saw

A lightweight bow saw is an efficient tool for cutting wood also. Notch the log at the spot where you plan to cut by moving the saw gently back and forth until the depth of the cut will hold the blade. Always use a smooth back and forth motion for the most efficient cutting. If the saw jams, work it loose by rocking it gently up and down until the blade is free. A sideways movement with the saw usually results in a broken blade. Your saw should have a cap or cover to fit over the saw teeth when it is not in use.

Other Tools

Here are some other tools you will be using in campcrafting:

For Making Wood Articles:

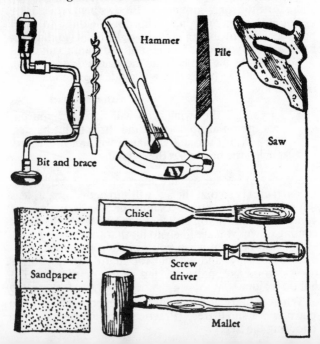

Bit and brace

Hammer

File

Saw

Chisel

Sandpaper

Screw driver

Mallet

For Woodpiles:

Sawbench

Bow Saw

Chopping Block

For Tin Work:

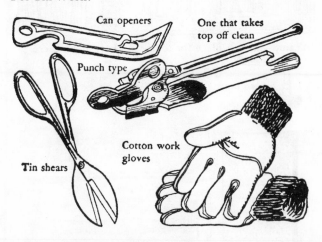

Can openers

One that takes top off clean

Punch type

Tin shears

Cotton work gloves

For Sharpening Tools:

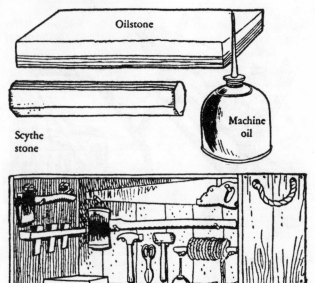

In camp—have a place for tools, and keep them there.

Things to Make with Knife or Axe

Use natural woods for pins, buckles, buttons, letter openers. Carve with knife; finish with fine sandpaper and polishing wax to bring out the grain of the wood.

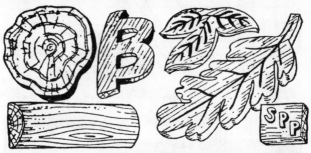

Pins of plain, polished wood, carved initial, favorite leaves

Dig out back; put in small safety pin with plastic wood. Smooth off and let harden.

Belt buckles   Napkin Ring   **Buttons of**
                         or Tie Slide   **wood or nuts**

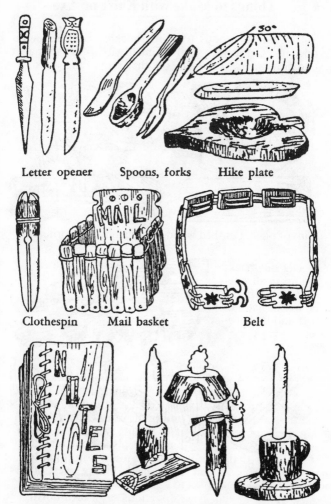

Letter opener   Spoons, forks   Hike plate

Clothespin   Mail basket   Belt

Notebook covers   Candlesticks

10
FINDING YOUR WAY

Do you know how to get around? Around outdoors, we mean. Can you tell directions by the sun and stars? Can you use a compass? A campcrafter uses the sun, stars, or compass as tools to help him in his campcrafting and hiking. Perhaps you will want the rising sun to peek into your tent. Perhaps you will want to place your tent so the east winds that usually bring rain are not going to enter the front. If you have been hiking west all morning, it may be helpful to know how to go back east to reach home. If your road directions say "turn north at the end of road," you may wish you knew in which direction north lies.

Anywhere, anytime —if you do know north, you can find the other directions easily. Face *north*, and *east* is at your right; *west* is at your left; *south* is in back of you. At noon your shadow points north.

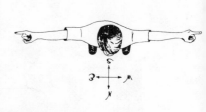

By the Sun

(This gives you general directions, not specific or accurate ones.) In the morning the sun is in the *east*; in the afternoon, in the *west*; and at noon, overhead, slightly toward the south.

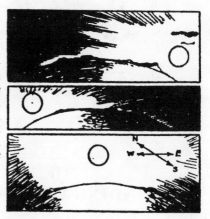

If you stand with your right shoulder toward the sun in the morning, or with your left shoulder toward the sun in the afternoon, you will be facing *north*, and *south* is in back of you. Your shadow will fall east or west, in the opposite direction.

By Your Watch

(This is more accurate.)

1. Hold watch level in the sun.

2. Hold a twig or blade of grass over the center point of the watch, so a shadow falls on face.

3. Slowly turn the watch until the shadow lies over the hour hand. North is the point halfway between the hour hand, as it then points, and the twelve on the face of the watch—one way in the morning, the other way in the afternoon.

By the Stars

At night the North Star will tell you where north is. Get someone to help you find the constellation known as the Big Dipper. The two "pointers" of this dipper always point to the Pole Star, or North Star. Face it, and you can find the other directions. Seafaring men used this star to steer their ships in olden days.

By a Compass

A compass is a watch-like instrument which has a magnetized needle that always points to the north. (Ask a science teacher to explain why.) There are many kinds of compasses—the very intricate and accurate mariners'

or engineers' compasses, and the very simple kind that you can get at many stores. Many compasses have a stationary printed face, something like a watch. The points of the compass are printed on the face. A needle with an arrow or point on one end swings on a peg in the center. Some have a dial on which the needle is fastened, and the whole compass face swings around.

To use a compass with a needle:

1. Face the object or direction you want to know about.
2. Hold compass in front of you, level, so needle swings freely.
3. The needle will swing back and forth, and finally come to rest. It then points north. The needle will wiggle and never be exactly still.
4. Now turn the compass carefully (the needle will stay in same position) until the N (or sometimes a spearhead) printed on the face of the compass is under the needle. This is called "orienting the compass," and makes the face point in the right direction. You control the compass face, but you cannot control the needle—it points north.

The compass face generally has a mark that shows north clearly; if it does not, figure out by the sun where north is, and you can tell how your own compass is marked.

5. Keep compass in this oriented position, and point a twig or pencil from edge of compass toward the object or direction. The end of the twig at the compass edge will point to the direction of the object or path. This is called "sighting with a compass." (If the needle and dial swing together, you will skip step 4.)

Take care of your compass—it is a delicate instrument, and should be handled with care if you hope to keep it accurate. If it has a way of locking the needle, so it does not swing freely when not in use, be sure to use it. Many compasses have cases that close, like a watch; this case protects the glass, and is good to have.

The directions given here are for the simplest type of compass, one that is relatively inexpensive and available in many stores. Another popular type of compass is the Silva compass, one used in orienteering. It has a base that makes it very easy to use.

When you progress to going cross-country, or mountain climbing, you may want to own and use a Silva compass. Perhaps a friend has one, and will help you learn to use it.

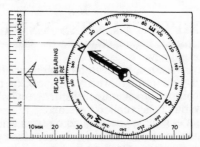

Reading and making maps may be good skills for you to learn next. Learn to use topographical maps. Trailing and cross-country hiking make use of direction-finding, too, and will be good fun. Orienteering is a sport that combines all of these skills and is growing in popularity.

11
CAMPING PLACES AND GEAR

Some day, we hope, you will have a chance to go camping—with your family, with your club, or to a day or resident camp, for several weeks or the whole summer. You may have the fun of developing a campsite with some other campers; you may go on trips where you will make or use temporary shelters and cooking places; you may sleep in tents or cabins that are all ready for you when you arrive. Wherever and however you camp, good care of your equipment and careful use of the environment are signs of good campcrafting.

An Outdoor Kitchen

Perhaps your first camping place will be in your yard, or some other spot near home, where the first thing you will make will be an outdoor kitchen. At a summer camp your tent or cabin group may develop such a kitchen near your living quarters, so it will be fun and easy to cook out as often as you want to plan it. Wherever your outdoor kitchen, you will want these things in it:

—*A cooking place*—Storage places for equipment and for food if you keep staple things such as sugar, salt, and so on.

—*A woodpile*

— *A table or work space*—A drain for dishwater and other liquids.

Those are the first things; you may want to add a cupboard, a cup-tree, a pan-tree, another fireplace, such as a reflector for baking.

Kitchen Equipment

A cupboard for dishes, kettles, salt, sugar and the like may be made of packing boxes or built to order. Here is a good portable one. The front lets down to make a work table. Cover the top with waterproof material.

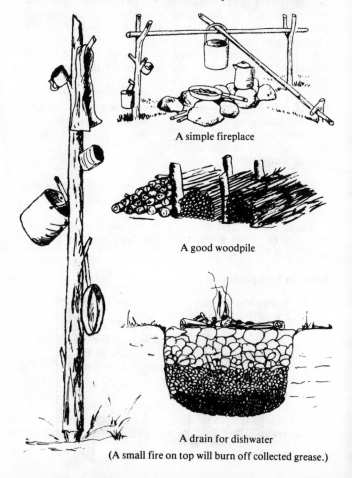

A simple fireplace

A good woodpile

A drain for dishwater
(A small fire on top will burn off collected grease.)

Perhaps your kitchen will look something like this:

Whether you camp in tents or cabins, part of your campcrafting will be to know about the shelter, how to take care of it and how to keep it in good condition.

If you live in tents, you may learn these things:

1. Types of tents, the various parts, and uses of the parts.
2. Knots used in erecting a tent or keeping it trim.
3. How to roll and tie flaps or tent walls.
4. How to take care of canvas, or nylon, wet or dry.
5. How to pitch a tent, peg it down; how to make it look "trim," and how to strike it.
6. How to put up mosquito tents or netting.
7. Here are some helps for wall tents, which are the usual kind found in resident camps; learn about your own type of tent.

Here are some helps for wall tents, which are the usual kind found in resident camps; learn about your own type of tent.

1. Some good things to know about canvas:
   —*Pins in canvas make holes* for the rain to come through and may start rips.
   —*Running the finger or foot down the roof* of the tent when it is wet will break the air bubbles that make the canvas waterproof, causing leaks.
   —*Canvas mildews when rolled up damp.* After a rain, let the sides and flaps dry before rolling them again.
   —*Field mice like to live in tents, too.* Watch your tent flaps in a long spell of pleasant weather; unroll them, and let them air once in a while.
   —*Canvas and ropes shrink when wet*, so ropes should be loosened at the beginning of a storm, and tightened again afterwards. Pull ropes evenly on both sides to keep the tent looking trim.
   —*The tent should fit loosely* when dry, so the sides may be pegged down to floor or floor pegs easily.

2. Nails may split tent poles—use lashings. Remove lashings before folding tents away.

3. When folding tents, be sure the material is dry. Let sun shine on it for two hours after dew has disappeared. Fold on seams smoothly. Brush cobwebs, insects, duff, and dirt off tent before folding.

If you live in a cabin at camp, you may learn these things:
   —How to care for whatever equipment is there— screens, curtains, shutters, etc., in sunny, wet or windy weather; how to roll and tie canvas screens; or how to fasten shutters.
   —How to put up shelves in a good craftsman-like manner. Make wooden pegs instead of using nails for hanging clothes.

—How to put up mosquito tents over your bed.
—How to make shoe racks, suitcase racks, etc.
—In log cabins, how to keep the chinking in good
  repair.

Camping Shelters

You may make a camp in your yard. Your family may
have a tent, and all of you may go off for a fine camping
holiday, you may go to a resident camp, or your troop
or group may own or borrow equipment for camping.
There are many kinds of camping shelters, from the pup
tent, erected for just a night or two, to big wall tents put
up for the summer at a camp.

"Pup" Tent

Poncho Shelter

Umbrella Tent

A-type Backpack Tent

In a summer camp, you may live in a large wall tent.

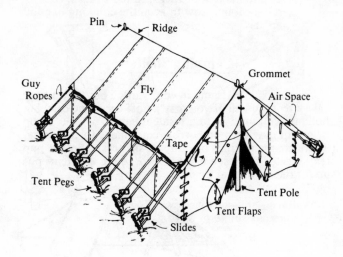

A WALL TENT with parts named
(Erected with tent pegs)

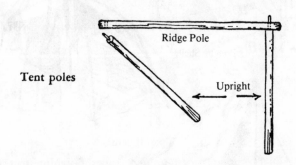

Tent poles

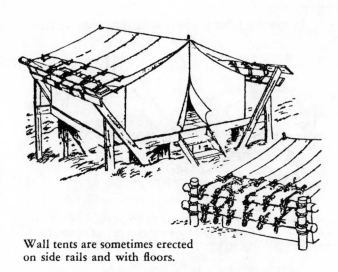

Wall tents are sometimes erected
on side rails and with floors.

To roll tent:

Unlace corner ropes; unhook ropes fastening tent to
ground pegs. Roll sides, rolling the edge inside, away

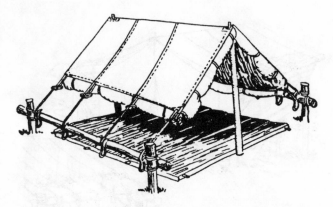

from you. Fold front flaps in on corners; roll inside and tie tapes with square knots. Tie tapes with square knots close to roof of tent. (Add tapes at seams if there are none.)

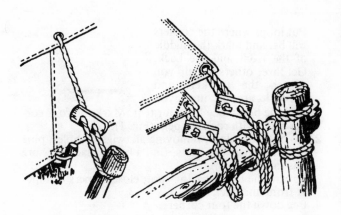

Tents are erected by pegs or on siderails. The wooden handle is to tighten or loosen ropes.

How to Pitch a Small Tent

When you go on an overnight camp, you'll need some kind of shelter for sleeping and for your personal gear. This will usually be a small, lightweight tent for one or two campers. Learn to pitch your tent before you take off on your trip; practice pitching it, striking it, rolling and tying it. Check to be sure there are no rips, all guy ropes are in good condition, and that you have the right number of poles and pegs.

Here's how to pitch a tent with a sewn-in floor:

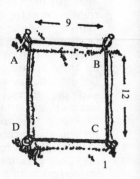

1. Make a marker of twine, the size of the floor of the tent.

Put loops where the corners will be, and mark the middle of the front and the back. Get three others to help you stretch the marker, and move it around until you 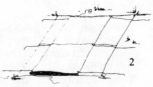 find the best place for your tent. Mark the four corner spots with rocks or pegs (Fig. 1).

2. Go over this place, removing all twigs, pebbles, pine cones. If there are roots, find a better place. Be sure it is smooth.

3. Spread the tent over the spot; close zippers or tapes at front and back (Fig. 2).

4. Peg down the four corners.

5. If you have poles and inside ridge, assemble these (Fig. 3). Undo zippers or tapes. Place poles inside tent, pins of upright poles in grommets in tent ridge, or through ridge pole, then in grommets.

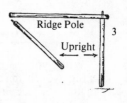

   If you do not have an inside ridge, place along front and back guy lines over pins of upright poles at top of tent.

6. With a person at each upright, raise tent placing upright poles at center of front and back. If the thent has ridge, stretch corner guy lines at angles to tent, and place on pegs (Fig. 4). If it has no ridge, stretch front and back guy lines and place pegs (or you may be able to tie lines to trees). If your tent has a "T" ridge, one person holds in place inside tent until front guy and

corner guys are in place.

7. Place pegs at side of tent, with guy lines in place. Be sure they are in line with corner pegs (Fig. 5). If there are no guy lines, peg tent at edge of floor. Adjust guy lines with slides or taut line hitches. Be sure the pull is the same on both sides of tent.

8. If the tent has a fly, place it on the pins of upright poles and raise with tent. Place pegs and guy lines with those for tent, making sure there is an air space between tent and fly. (Fig.7). You may use pegs with two notches for a tent and fly. (Fig.8).

9. Stand out in front of tent, and check to be sure it is trim and square—no wrinkles, no pulls, poles straight. You'll probably need to do some adjusting.

10. Rope will tighten when wet from dew or rain, and be slack when it dries. You will need to check often to be sure guy lines are taut.

   If your tent does not have a sewn-in floor, measure the floor space carefully, put pegs in the four corner spots, and proceed as above.

Place your tent so the morning sun shines into it—on a knoll, if possible, so rain will run off.

How to Strike a Tent

To strike a tent, here are a few suggestions:

1. Be sure the tent is dry.
2. Take out all pegs except corner and front and back pegs.
3. With a camper at each upright pole, drop the tent and remove the poles and ridge, if there is one.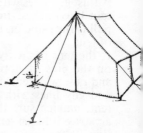
4. Take up all remaining pegs.
5. If it is a small tent, pick up by ridge and corners, and shake to remove grass, leaves, or insects. If large, spread out on ground and brush each surface.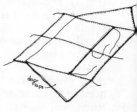
6. Smooth tent, top and underneath, and spread doors out to side.
7. Fold tent in on seams and doors, then walls and ground cloths and floor, folding into a small rectangle. If you have a bag for the tent, make the folds so that tent will fit into bag. Fold guy ropes, loose, inside tent, except for one corner guyline.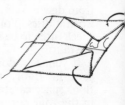
8. Fold and roll tent, and tie with the corner guy line. Brush tent as each surface is folded on top.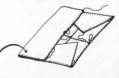

9. Clean pegs; be sure they are
   dry, and place in peg bag.
   Include bag and sectional poles
   inside.

When you live in a summer camp tent or cabin, make
it comfortable.

Shelf for a tent, for sweaters,
bathrobes, etc.

A clothes drier made from a
small, dead cedar tree.

A bureau from a box or an
orange crate. You may not want
a curtain in snake country.

A box on casters for under the
bed.

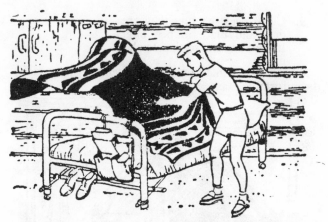

A shoe bag holds all odd bits of equipment in handy fashion.

A good camper covers his pillow and sheets with a dark blanket to keep them dry and clean.

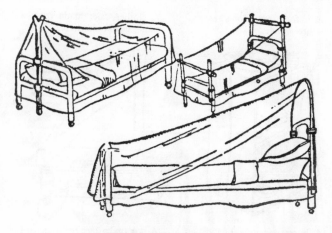

Mosquito Netting Frames.

YOUR OWN BOOK OF CAMPCRAFT

Seats and stools for tent or campfire circle.

A wastebasket of lashed twigs.   A broom made of twigs.   A sundial on a log.

Letters for signs of twigs or blocks of wood.

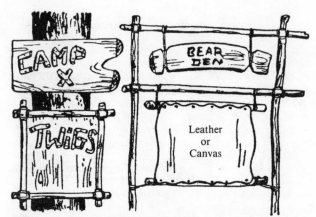

Bulletin boards or signposts.

Showers or bath shelters.

Setting Up Camp for Your First Overnight

When you have had several day hikes and have learned the basic campcraft skills, you will want to put them all to good use by camping overnight. This will expand your food planning to several meals and add the fun of providing shelters to your campcrafting.

When you plan that first overnight with your group, you will need help from a camping expert in how to choose a site, set it up with shelters, cooking area, and sanitary facilities. If your tent or cabin group from a resident camp is making the plans, you may be able to use an outpost area on the camp property or a nearby site arranged by the camp. If it is an in-town group, you may find organizational facilities or state park areas available. Your first overnight camp may not be at a completely primitive site where you must provide everything, but you can work up to that.

Wherever you go, you will need to check out the site beforehand to learn what is provided, what your camp group must provide, and how you get to use the site. Here are items for you to examine:

The Site: Is there a shelter you can use in an emergency like a downpour in the middle of the night? If so, you may be able to sleep out under the stars without tents. You may plan to use small tents for sleeping and for storing personal gear. If so, practice pitching the tents before your trip. Check to be certain the tents are in good condition.

Choose open level ground for tents or sleeping areas, preferably on a rise, so rain will run off and not gather under sleeping bags. Avoid areas under large trees, near swamps and marshes, or on sand, which has an unpleasant way of getting into everything.

Face your tents so the morning sun will shine into them and so rains and winds will strike one side and back.

Make use of natural resources such as rocks for fire-places, good drainage possibilities, fuel and water supply.

Make note of the terrain and plan accordingly for fire circles, sanitary facilities, and program possibilities. Are there minor hazards such as cliffs, many dead branches, or swamps? Are there possibilities of major hazards such as flash floods? Each site will have some hazards; learn about them and plan accordingly.

Cooking Areas: Are there established fireplace areas you must use, as in a state park? You will need cooking fires and fires to heat water; work space for preparing meals and doing dishes, and fuel; facilities for disposal of garbage, liquids, other refuse. There may be containers provided; you may be able to burn some refuse; you may have to carry out non-burnables. Burying garbage and tin cans is no longer acceptable in camping or wilderness areas.

Plan your meals with consideration of the cooking facilities provided or those you must establish. For your first overnights, plan menus that are simple to cook, that are easily prepared, and that take little fuel. One cooked item each meal is a good way to start.

Is there wood available for fires, or must you carry in wood or charcoal briquets or a stove?

Sanitary Facilities: Are latrines provided? If so, how will you take care of them and leave them in good condition? If not, what will you plan for primitive latrines, and how will you leave them on your departure?

Is there a water supply for drinking, cooking, personal and dish washing, fire protection? If not, how will you get a water supply that is safe for drinking and cooking, and ample for washing? Are drains provided, or must you make drains for waste liquids? If you camp by a lake or brook, you may use the water for washing, but must purify it for drinking and cooking.

How will you take care of waste liquids, garbage, non-burnable refuse?

Wood Supply: Is there wood for fires for cooking, for heating, for burning garbage, for campfires? Can you find sticks for constructing cranes or work areas or poles for tents? If you *can* use wood on the site for fuel, be sure to leave a good woodpile for the next campers.

Tools: Talk over what you will need to set up your site—shovels for digging, a saw for cutting wood.

Packing Gear: Learn to pack your personal gear so you can carry it on your back. Go light! Take just what you will need for your short stay.

Plan group gear so it can be assembled and packed efficiently. You'll need to pitch tents, make a cooking area, store food before it gets dark. Divide gear so each person carries some group gear as well as personal gear.

Emergencies: Talk about what might happen, and plan to meet such emergencies. They will differ with each camping site. Know how to get help if needed. Be sure someone at home can be contacted if you have an emergency, or are delayed in returning.

Plan fire protection at each fire site.

Plan for adequate first aid.

What will you do?: On an overnight, the activity will mainly consist of setting up camp, making it comfortable, constructing simple facilities, cooking and eating—and just sitting around talking. Take needed equipment for other planned program—compasses, knives and sharpening stones for whittling, ropes to practice new knots. You'll want to explore, hike, play outdoor games.

When You Leave?: Leave the site in better condition than you found it. Do something to improve the conservation of the site. Fill in all holes and drains. Clean out fireplaces, or leave fire areas with no trace they have been there. Put fires out as soon as you have finished using them, so you'll be sure they are out when you leave.

Pack as carefully for the return trip as you did when you started out. Arrange for cleanup and return of equipment you have used, and for taking care of leftover food and supplies.

12
OUTDOOR MANNERS

Did you every try to find a place for a picnic lunch, stopping at several spots only to find litters of papers and orange peels and bottles? Did you ever watch a farmer try to get his straying cows back in a pasture, after someone hadn't bothered to close a gate? Did you ever see a boy poking a snake with a stick just to make it wiggle? Did you ever—but you need not be reminded of people with poor outdoor manners. There are those who forget their manners when they get out into the open, and there are those who treat people and things and places with a courtesy that shows appreciation. Camp-

crafters, of course, are familiar with good outdoor
behavior and manners.

There is more to outdoor behavior than just good
manners; there is the angle of good, sensible safety and
care, and of not taking chances that will make it
difficult for you or for other people. Call it manners or
behavior, or citizenship—it all adds up to the way you
act when you are out. Good campcrafters have a code
for such behavior; like all good manners, the code
begins with thinking of others and acting as you would
like others to act toward you or your property.

Getting About

When you walk by yourself, you have little difficulty
getting along without disturbing someone else. When
you go hiking or walking with a group, you present
another picture; you present greater difficulties to car
drivers or to pedestrians. So it is well to know some
rules of the road that will help you all get where you
want to go, and to get there by the simplest, safest way.
Here are some hints:

On sidewalks, break up into twos and threes, and
don't spread across so that people coming in the opposite
direction can't get by.

At crosswalks, wait together for a light to change, or
for a chance to cross. Don't straggle across.

Along a highway, walk on the left, facing traffic, in
twos or threes, dropping behind each other in a single
line if oncoming traffic needs to come close.

At night, wear something white like an armband, or
carry a flashlight.

When with leaders, have one at the front and one at
the end of the line. Put those with the shortest legs in
front. Or let the long-legged hikers go on ahead in one
group.

Don't thumb rides.

On buses and trains keep together, and remember that the other people in the bus may not wish to be "entertained" by your songs, cheers and screams. When your private bus goes through city streets, you are in the public eye. Save your singing until you are out on the open road.

When riding bicycles, know and obey traffic regulations.

Out in the Country

Leave things as you find them—or leave them improved.

Be sure to leave gates closed or open, as you find them. This is very important to the farmer.

Get permission to go on private property.

Stick to paths when going across farm land, especially fields of hay or grain; go around the edges of fields when there is no path.

Apples on trees, cucumbers on vines, flowers in yards are all private property! Some people think anything that grows is public property.

Except when you know how to go across country, keep to trails in the woods. Leave trail signs and markers as you find them, unless you help put them in better condition for other hikers.

Check back to the notes on fire building and fire safety, and be sure you know how to put them into practice.

Leave trunks of trees and wooden walls and fences without the benefit of your initials or other whittlings.

Don't strip bark from living trees.

Leave your picnic site or campsite as you wish you had found it—clean, no rubbish, no garbage, a supply of fuel for the next fellow.

Live and let live—don't kill or harm or bother or needlessly destroy things and creatures that grow in the open.

Help make your yard or your camp a wildlife sanctuary, where birds and animals find shelter and food—and friends.

Safety Outdoors

Watch out for water—carry it with you in a canteen, or get it from a public supply, or make it pure with some purifying agent.

If you are in unfamiliar territory, plan to get back to your camp or home well before dark.

If you are lost—don't get panicky; try to think out where you have come from, by the sun or a compass, and go back in the opposite direction. Go down hill rather than up. Following a brook will generally lead to some home or farm or village.

When with a group—have partners and do not go so far from the main group that you cannot hear shouts or a whistle. Have prearranged signals—and stick by them.

If one person is hurt, and another goes for help, leave the hurt person as warm and comfortable as possible. Mark the trail well on the way back to camp or the group.

For skiing, canoeing, bicycling and other means of travel, learn first aid, accident prevention, repairs to equipment, etc., before starting out on the trip.

It will all add up to good manners again—don't take chances that may mean that many people will have to risk their lives to help you because you didn't pay attention or didn't stick with the others.

Good campcrafters—good outdoor friends!

13
OUR PIONEER HERITAGE

Our parents' grandmothers may have told them true stories of the days when they were little girls, traveling west with their families in covered wagons; their grandfathers may have told of helping to homestead some territory; your forefathers may have been members of Indian tribes on the Great Plains. All of them were the campers of olden days. They left us a heritage of living out-of-doors, of adventures, of sound bodies and resourceful heads and hands. We can catch the spirit and learn much from books and stories that tell of their ways of life, their struggles, and their accomplishments. We can follow the great scouts like Kit Carson and Davy

Crockett; we can go afield with Sacajawea; we can travel the Oregon Trail in a covered wagon; we can live again with the Pilgrims in the log huts of the earliest settlements on this continent. You can find books that tell of the settling of your particular part of the country. Series such as "The Rivers of America" tell the tales of people who ventured forth to find new homes in new territories.

There was plenty of adventure in the lives of early settlers; there was good outdoor living, too. They cooked over improvised fireplaces; they made their own utensils of wood or shells or clay or gourds; they learned to make and use tools to simplify their living; they discovered food in the woods and fields and streams; they grew their food, too. They lived by their wits, their strength, and their resourcefulness. The children of these families learned early to take their part in the living. From their adventures and their practical living, the camper of today gains much to make his camping good.

Books can help you catch this spirit of the pioneers, early settlers, Indians, cowboys and trailblazers. Look in your public library and on shelves of today's paperbacks to find such tales. Eric Sloane's, *Diary of an American Boy*, (Wilfred Funk, Inc., 1962) is such a story.

You may find books that tell of the crafts that early settlers used. Many such crafts are still popular today, and many are part of our outdoor activities. Pioneer fathers made toys for their children; pioneer boys learned to whittle as soon as they could handle jack knives. They made their own games and their own entertainment.

Songs and dances, too, are part of our heritage from those early days. You probably know many of the folk songs from today's folk singers and from the musicians who play fiddles, dulcimers, recorders, or guitars. Perhaps you play some such instrument and are helping to keep alive the songs of generations ago. If you like to square dance or to play singing games, which are the simplest dances, you are enjoying part of our heritage. Square and round dances were holiday and evening fun for young people in early settlements. Today there are many young groups that meet regularly to dance these dances. Your physical education teacher may be able to help you find books and records that will help you start such a group in town, or enjoy such activities in camp.

14
ALL OUTDOORS

Lakes, hills, forests, plains, streams or deserts—all these may be the starting place for your hiking and camping—the whole outdoors. Whatever you do, wherever you go, Mother Nature has many treasures in store for you, if you are interested, if you are curious, if you have imagination. There is no part of camping that is not linked with nature; campcrafters learn to know what is around them, and how it can serve them for usefulness and for pleasure. Wonderful new trails are open to you when you begin to stop, look, and listen to the world around you.

Everything you handle, everything you use, in camp or otherwise, comes from nature—the pencil with which you write, the paper this book is printed on, the chair on which you are sitting, and the food you had for lunch. As you become aware of the out-of-doors, you begin to learn how dependent one thing is upon other things; you begin to realize what remarkable resources are found in nature. And then you find yourself learning something about a very important problem—conservation.

There is much talk now about the need for conserving our natural resources in this country, and in the world. This is not idle talk, but it grows from a realization that carelessness and wastefulness have destroyed so much of our forests and lands and streams and wildlife that there is much to be concerned about. You may not think that you can do much about preventing a flood or the erosion of land, or about stopping a big forest fire. But there are things that you can do, in your own small way, for a good camper is a conservationist. He is frugal with what is plentiful, taking just what he needs, and he protects what is rare, leaving it or helping it to grow. A campcrafter does not needlessly kill anything—an insect on the path or a deer in the woods. He does not slash trees and pull up flowers. He knows that each living thing has a place and each helps to keep the balance of all things that grow.

When you are a good campcrafter, you are a good conservationist, too. The following pledge is now widely accepted and used by organizations and individuals interested in conserving our natural heritage:

> *I give my
> pledge as an American
> to save and faithfully to
> defend from waste the
> natural resources of
> my country—its soil
> and minerals, its
> forests, waters,
> and wildlife.*

When you cut a sapling, consider how you can help other trees to grow by your cutting; when you make a path up a hill, make it a zigzag path rather than straight up and down, so you will keep rains from washing away the soil; when you build fires outdoors, be extra careful so you are never guilty of starting a forest fire—these are ways you can help America keep her natural resources to serve your grandchildren and their grandchildren.

Nature serves many uses in campcrafting; it also leads the way to many hobbies or life professions. The scientists of today were the boys and girls of yesterday who liked learning about flowers or stones or insects or birds. There are many, many adults today who find great joy in some hobby that is based on birdlore or rock-finding or wild flowers. A campcrafter's enjoyment of the out-of-doors is based on a general appreciation of the whole outdoors, of the beauty of the countryside, of the interesting things that are in the out-of-doors.

Do not feel that you must be an expert to enjoy nature. Begin by just looking around you at what is growing, what is on the land, what is in the sky, and what is in the water. Soon you will begin to see the same things over again, and you will find that you know a few names. There are books to help in every step—very simple ones that help you begin to know, and more technical ones to help when you have progressed along the nature trail.

Start by getting acquainted. If you see someone you never knew before, or if a friend says, "Say, you'd like to meet so-and-so," you answer: "What's his name? Where is he from? What's he like?" The same thing is true in meeting a bird or a flower or a tree—find out these same three things, name—where it lives—what it is like. Soon you will feel you have met an old friend when that bird flashes by, or you pass that tree, or you find that flower again.

Try to find someone who is already interested in nature to share his/her enthusiasm with you; if you are in camp, there will be counselors who are interested; if you are with a group, your leader may be able to find someone who would like to talk with you; there is undoubtedly someone on your own block who has a garden, knows about snails or toads, or is a stargazer.

Don't try everything at once. Begin looking, admiring, protecting things in general, and soon you will discover what phase of nature lore you like best. But do not expect to complete everything in short order. Some men spend their lives learning about one small part of one of nature's classifications and still feel they have much more to learn. Most of us do not go that far—we just like certain things, and learn something more about them. It isn't so much learning names and other information as it is learning to enjoy and appreciate nature.

One wonderful thing about nature is that it is all around, everywhere—all year through, in the city or the country; another is that it is free. There is no price of admission to watch a mother bird feeding her babies, to watch the clouds overhead, to lie on pine needles and look up through the branches, or to cool your feet in a brook and watch the water striders busily at work.

There are all sorts of things to do that will help you learn about nature; this one short chapter can only point out some trail markers to you; you can find people and other books to help you—but to begin, here are some ideas:

—Get acquainted with your neighbors—the things that grow near your home, your tent, or the hill where you picnic. Learn about your own particular part of the country; nature varies in every section.

—Learn to identify any poisonous plants or animals in your locality. Learn what they do, how they do it, and then you can learn how to avoid difficulties with them. Many are not as bad as they seem when you know how to deal with them or how to avoid them.

—Some people like to make lists, collect pictures, make notebooks or diaries. Others prefer gardens or bird feeding stations, or similar activities.

—There are many stories and poems about the out-of-doors, and about things that live there.

—Wood is a great campcrafting material—you will want to learn about it, how to use it well, why some is hard, some straight, and why some burns well.

—Stones, too, will serve you—you will use them for

fireplaces and may discover that some blow up or are not very useful. You will want to know why.

—Weather is always with us—there are many interesting activities in forecasting the weather.

—If you have a camera, there are all sorts of new trails to follow in taking pictures in the out-of-doors.

—There are things to make—birdhouses and gourd dishes, and things to sketch or paint.

Whether you like birds, beasts, or fowl; whether you take an interest in the vegetable, animal, or mineral kingdom; whether you make bird and flower lists; or whether you enjoy nature by observation—you will always be grateful for all of nature, and all of the out-of-doors that makes camping possible. And, we hope, you will be a good outdoor citizen as well.

If you are interested in getting good information and help, and if you would like to share a small part in the big job of protecting wildlife in this country, get in touch with one of these organizations to find out about club or individual memberships:

—The National Audubon Society, 950 Third Avenue, New York, NY 10022

—Sierra Club, P.O. Box 7959, Rincon Annex, San Francisco, CA 94120

—National Wildlife Federation, 1412-16th Street N.W., Washington, D.C. 20036

Books You Will Enjoy

There are so many books on nature and conservation that it is difficult to recommend just a few. Ask in your public or school library for any general or specialized nature books they have. There are many inexpensive books that you may buy to build your own nature library; some are small and easily slipped in your knapsack or pocket. Get in the habit of looking at book racks and counters for nature books.

State and federal conservation, park, and forest services have numerous pamphlets which are generally free or cost only a few cents. Write to your own state bureau of information, or to the Superintendent of Documents, Washington 25, D.C., to find out what is available.

There are many camping books that will be good additions to your own library. They will help you go beyond the first steps shown in this book. As you advance along the camping trail, you will want to know more of camping.

15
AROUND THE CAMPFIRE

When you sit by the fire alone, you may want the companionship of a good book; when you sit around a campfire, you look for the companionship of other campers. Books and people are the right companions for armchair camping or for real camping. Sometimes you want one, sometimes the other; sometimes you combine them both in the plans you have for a campfire, or for the unplanned, spontaneous things that happen around a campfire.

We have suggested that there is much of pioneer lore to help you know and enjoy outdoor living; there are hundreds of other books that you will enjoy, too; for any good yarn, any good song, any poem of the out-of-doors will add to the fellowship of a campfire. You will soon find favorite anthologies or collections or individual books that seem to make your camping equipment complete. Here are a few suggestions of books that campers like:

—Stories of men and women who have camped or traveled in canoes, in boats, on horseback, or on foot to unexplored country or little known lands.

—Nature stories—tales of the creatures that live in the woods, the fields, the streams, or stories of the people who have found adventure in fossil beds, on mountainsides, in rivers or lakes, as they discovered the wonders of the natural world.

—Stories that are the folklore of our country—the tall tales of Paul Bunyan or the record of the wandering Johnny Appleseed.

—Stories that tell of the settling of the various sections of our country—the American Mountain series, the Rivers of America series, and others.

—Stories of the people who have lived and worked in the out-of-doors—Indians and sailors, cowboys and lumbermen.

—Nature poems and poems of the open are favorites with campers. There are anthologies that slip easily into pocket or knapsack; many campers like to make their own collections of poems that seem to describe a favorite spot or some happening on the trail.

Songs, too, are expressions of our feelings. There are songs for hiking, songs for quiet moments, songs that tell of the out-of-doors and of the people who have lived there. There are the songs we make up to tell our own adventures. There are songs that can be acted out, story songs, ceremonial songs, work songs. There are songs that describe outdoor things and outdoor feelings. Any good song is a good camping song, but some that have hiking rhythm or that fit into outdoor living seem to serve the campcrafter best.

It's dusk—night is beginning to creep in—the fire lighter steps forward to touch off the blaze that will make the flames leap high. Everyone leans forward a little, in great anticipation of the nicest part of the camp day—campfire time. If there are just a few of you, you may build up the dying cooking fire, stretch out around it to tell stories, sing a bit, or just sit and watch the flames. Campfires are the frosting of camping; you will always remember the evenings in camp.

What happens at campfires? Well, almost anything, and there is no specified kind of program. Some are very informal, with nothing at all planned; some are ceremonials, with much preparation. In between are nights of fun which may include:

Singing—in small and large groups, or by one person. Rollicking songs, ballads, rounds, part songs, and quiet ones.

Music—especially with the instruments that help group singing or that are easily transported.

Dramatics—plays, ceremonies, informal and impromptu stunts, dramatized stories, poems and songs, puppets, pantomimes, etc.

Stories and yarns—told by a storyteller, improvised by members of the group, read by someone; chronicles of the day's adventures.

Games—guessing games, quiet games, trailing games, games that match wits, stunts that match strength, pencil and paper games.

Talks and pictures—by campers, foresters, and naturalists who share their knowledge and their enthusiasm. Sometimes pictures add to their talks.

Discussions—planned or unplanned—on any subject.

Sometime when you are on a camping trip, you will probably find others to share with you the peace of a campfire; at a mountain shelter you might meet someone whose harmonica just makes you sing; at a forest campsite there could be someone who has had some real adventures in the out-of-doors; and at a big campfire at a summer camp you might discover the joy of letting your own voice join in the singing of a crowd. Wherever it is, whatever you do, you will find the trail of camping has no equal in companionship, adventure, and sheer fun. It will mean the completing of a hike, the cooking out, the learning to use a knife or an axe, the planning, the work, and fun that have gone into your own camp-crafter's trail—and you will know that you will always be following a trail wherever you are, whatever you do.

16
WHAT'S IT CALLED?

Camping, like every special interest, has specific terms that are used to describe objects or acts; a good campcrafter knows and uses such words. He doesn't "put up" a tent, he "pitches" it. He packs his "gear" for a trip. He know that "ticks" and "flies" are not insects.

Here are a few camping terms—add others as you learn them.

1) Gear—equipment, both personal and group.

Hike kit—a small, over-the-shoulder pack for day trips, for personal gear. Generally made of lightweight material. A beginner's piece of gear.

Knapsack—a small, heavier pack, worn on the shoulder or on the back.

Pack (or backpack)—a larger, heavier pack, usually with a wooden or metal frame—worn on the back.

Backpacking means carrying all your gear for a camp or for mountain climbing.

Blanket roll—a sleeping bag made of folded blankets.

Sleeping bag—a ready-made bag, lined with dacron or down, etc.

Ground sheet or cloth—a waterproof sheet of plastic or rubberized material. Placed under sleeping bag on the ground.

Poncho—a rectangular waterproof with an opening for head in middle. Sometimes has grommets, and can be pitched like a tent. also used for a ground cloth.

Air mattress—a collapsible mattress which can be rolled into a small packet for carrying; it is blown up at camp.

Ticks—mattress bags made of burlap, ticking, etc., to be stuffed with leaves or straw at campsite—for long-term camps.

Ditty bags—cloth bags in many sizes, made of plastic, light canvas, unbleached cotton. Used to pack personal gear, food, tent pegs. Usually have circular bottoms. Large ditty bags may hold all your gear for a long-term camp.

Duffle bag—a heavy canvas bag for personal or group gear for long-term camping. Has straps and handle for carrying.

2) Shelters

Tent—an outdoor room and roof. Comes in many shapes and sizes, made of many kinds of materials. Portable, lightweight tents are used for overnight and short-term camps; heavier, larger tents for long-term and summer camps.

Pitch—to erect a tent.

Strike—to take down and fold a tent.

Fly—some tents have an extra "roof" for protection from rain and the heat of the sun, provided by an air space between tent and fly.

Tarp (or tarpaulin)—a rectangular or square sheet with tapes or rings—may be pitched in a variety of ways to form shelters or used as a ground cloth.

Poles—tent poles or uprights hold front and back of tent erect. May be wooden or metal. Sometimes come in sections. Tent poles have pins or spikes at top that fit into grommet or through ridge and tent.

Ridge poles—are wooden or metal strips that fit inside the top of the tent, to keep tent taut.
  —a "T" ridge is a short strip, with a partial hole in the middle into which one tent pole fits.
  —some tents will have frames of poles that fit inside or outside tent.
  —shears—poles used outside a tent, which is suspended on the cross piece, leaving inside of tent free of poles.

Guy ropes or lines—ropes that hold the tent in place with tent pegs. One end is fastened in grommet of tent, the other end with a loop knot over peg.

Grommet—a metal eyelet fastened in tent, for holding rope.

Slides—wooden or metal strips for tightening or loosening guy ropes.

Pegs—Wooden or metal strips that hold guy ropes, placed in ground at angle to tent, or at base of wall or ground cloth.

Sod Cloth—a strip of material sewed inside bottom of tent over which a ground cloth is placed.

Knots used in tent pitching:
  —*overhand* to secure rope in grommet
  —*bowline* to make a loop to slip over pole spike; will not move
  —*taut line hitch*—used on guy ropes—a loop that will move to loosen or tighten guys ropes.
  —*clove hitch*—used to secure guys to trees.

3) Outdoor Food

Nosebag or poke lunch—a hike lunch, ready to eat, carried in a bag, bandana or hike kit by individual hikers.

Non-utensil meal—meal prepared without pots or pans, but with natural materials, such as rocks, green sticks, broilers.

Foil cooking—in aluminum foil, a steaming or baking process. Foil may be cleaned and used again. (Carry home for disposal.)

One-pot meals—a hearty stew or casserole-type dish, all-in-one, supplemented by uncooked items.

4) Fires and Fireplaces

Cooking fireplaces—vary from simplest trench of logs, bricks, rocks, to reflector fires or fires in tin can stoves. Small fires or coals used for cooking.

Fire starters—made-at-home, carried in pack. Start easily from a match flame.

Buddy burners—wax and cardboard in small tin cans. Used as fuel in tin can stoves. (NOT for direct toasting or broiling).

Vagabond stoves—made of varied sizes of tin cans. Fuel may be twigs or charcoal.

Fuzz stick—whittled soft wood, with shavings left on stick—for starting fires.

Dingle or waugan sticks and cranes—sticks erected to hold pots over fire.

Campfire—large fire, usually in a fire ring, for group to gather around for evening programs. Sometimes lighted ceremoniously.

5) Fire Materials—wood or charcoal briquets

Tinder—dry, fine twigs, or shavings, which will light from a match. You need lots!

Kindling—sticks just larger than tinder, to catch from lighted tinder. Gradually increased in size to make a steady, well-burning fire. Makes water boil quickly.

Fuel—good sized sticks or logs that keep the fire burning, or charcoal briquets. Coals result when fuel has burned down, with no flames present. Best for toasting and broiling—worth waiting for.

6) Campsites

Primitive camping—when a group sets up a camp-site—shelters, sanitary facilities, cooking areas.

Latrine—an outdoor toilet, varying from a hole in the ground to a trench. Dirt from hole is used to cover contents after each use, and to fill in hole at end of stay. Seats may be lashed, and curtains hung for privacy.

7) Trail Kitchen Equipment

Drains—for waste liquids from cooking, personal or dish washing. Vary from simple deep hole to longer-term drains made of rocks.

Caches—storage places for dry or perishable foods. May be covered pails, boxes, bags. Coolers vary from boxes in brooks to moss-lined holes to tin cans cooled by evaporation. (They are coolers—not refrigerators.) Used to keep food from insects, animals and dust.

Dunk bags—light-weight bags made for individual camper's eating kit; used to dunk dishes in hot water after washing and rinsing. Hung on bushes or racks to dry.

What are some other camping terms you know?

List them here. Can you think of a good game for your group based on these terms?